Aunt Birdie's Chronicles

Adventures of a bondservant of the
Lord Jesus

Juanita Garrett McKimens

WinePress Publishing
MUKILTEO, WA 98275

Reviews

"Aunt Birdie's" story reflects the true molding by God's Grace. This author is indeed a natural motivator as seen by her growth in the many circumstances that have arisen in her walk with the Lord and how He has helped her handle them. She is a true inspiration and a model to be copied."

—*William L. Conner, MD, Ret.*

"Aunt Birdie is a woman of child-like faith who has experienced modern miracles. She has believed that God really means what He has promised. Ways she has responded to tough situations could only have been God-inspired.

For fifteen years Bissell Garrett, another bond-slave of the Lord, led in total dedication as they served Him together, in youth work, rescue missions and Hume Lake Christian camps. For five years they lovingly cared for needy children in Ireland. 'We can't take our houses and lands to Heaven,' he would say, 'but we can take boys and girls.'

After he had given all his earthly possessions and strength the Heavenly Father welcomed him home.

Aunt Birdie continued her faith walk through widowhood and a difficult second marriage proving God's keeping power and guidance. As she approaches 90, she hasn't retired. Read this inspiring account of the acts of Aunt Birdie."

—*Ray Johnson, Life Messengers Founder*

"Juanita McKimens has led a long and fruitful life. She has devoted herself to serving our Lord Jesus Christ in a wide variety of circumstances and settings. It is my hope that her account of her life will bring glory to our Lord and prompt others to serve Him."

—*Scott Gilchrist, Pastor*

Acknowledgments

To the many who have transferred my handwritten script to computer disk and have edited the manuscript, I offer deep gratitude.

To the late Dr. Douglas Smith, university professor, and Nick Marino in Guam who were devoted to the task of encouraging others to trust God as He led in my life.

To Sandy Dobish, Teri Beskow, Jon and Cecily Spencer, Mike and Janet Brand, Jerry Godfrey, Stephen Monaco and others who have helped me.

May God reward each one and bless those who read about what God has done in one life and will do for all who leave the controls with Him.

Juanita in the military, 1943.

Introduction

Adventure was part of God's plan for my life even before birth. Only God could devise a plot so complex resulting in His ultimate intentions being carried out in many lives.

Friends may find a very brief summary of the years of His basic training interesting as He was molding the life of this missionary.

It would take volumes to recount events of early experiences that eventually led to the greatest thrill of all my life and the fruit the Lord produced through half a century of service.

Summarizing the 32 years before "Aunt Birdie's Chronicles" begins: I was conceived in a sod house in the center of South Dakota. After gaining title to the homestead, Harvey and Mabel McComb traded it for a peach orchard in Colorado. Following trails across the Rosebud Indian Reservation they crossed the mountains on the Oregon Trail. They finally reached Grand Junction after riding in a lumber wagon over 300 miles. It was especially hard for my mother who was holding a yearling on her lap and a baby inside. They reached the orchard just in time for me to be born in a peach packing shed. Mother made it over into a home by building a kitchen and screen porch. Lenore came along two years later. Dad built a green house and cared for a garden and the orchard.

The only way to get the peaches to market was by train. When crooks got control of the shipping, after 4 years, the growers lost everything. We stayed with Dad's sisters until he got a job as horticulturist at the State Experiment Station near North Platte, Neb. Although dad had a green thumb and a brilliant mind, he never found contentment. His father died while he was a boy and his mother and older sisters spoiled him, causing him to be extremely selfish and hot tempered. Mother was the one who supplied most of our needs. Elaine and I carried heavy responsibilities while she taught school or art classes all day. The two years Dad had a farm, when I was in second and third grades, we worked to the point of exhaustion fearing his abuse.

I was ridiculed by him and his sisters because I was slow in school while my sisters got top grades with no effort. I was a junior in High School before my eyes were tested. When corrective glasses were provided I could see properly.

Those years that I was considered unintelligent were spent alone when possible studying the birds. I could imitate them so perfectly that some would even alight on me. It gave me a feeling of worth and Mother encouraged me in this hobby.

When Dad became too abusive, Mother took us to Greeley, Colo. and started an art studio. We helped by doing janitorial work and child care while attending school in 9th and 10th grades. In History class we were to report on some ancient people. Mother had been a missionary among the American Indians who lovingly gave her many beautiful gifts. I loved her stories and the meanings of the intricate designs. As I explained each article to the class I forgot all fear of rejection. That evening a classmate ran over waving a paper. "Look," she called "you got your name in the paper." There on the back of the front page was a full column. My teacher had written it up. Suddenly I was in demand to share with other classes. I became art editor of the school paper, on first team in basketball and debate team. That summer I attended Greeley State Teachers College and earned college credits that later helped me graduate from University in four years while earning all expenses.

After two years Dad begged Mother to return. He had turned over a "new leaf" and joined a church and started buying a home. Soon after we were reunited, we attended evangelistic meetings for two weeks. Elaine and I accepted the Savior and were baptized and joined the church. The last day an invitation was made for any who felt called to become missionaries. I went to the altar. I was sure God was speaking to me. I became very active in the church and zealous to share my faith. I observed so much hypocrisy among professing Christians that my heart was broken. Some I idolized failed me. While in High School a $25.00 prize was offered for a home talent show. Lying on my bed I planned an imaginary hike giving the calls and habits of many birds and farm animals. After winning the prize my "Bird Hike" and whistling solos were in demand.

During the great depression it was extra hard to earn my way through university and teacher's college but I was determined to convince my father that I could.My first school was out in the Sand Hills where I shared poverty with dear people who knew suffering. I was learning to endure hardness as a good soldier of Jesus Christ. I spent the next summer on Dude Ranch working for multimillionaires seeking something money couldn't buy.

After substitute teaching in High School, at the pastor's suggestion I offered my programs to the churches as a way of raising money. The offering was to be divided. I soon learned that those churches have no love for the Lord or the lost. I had many adventures that year that proved God's protection and provision for His wandering child. I gave the same Presentation in schools and felt I was leading people to love God through appreciation of His creation. I painted a dozen pictures of birds on silk set between green "trees" filling the stage. As I impersonated that bird it was illuminated.

The principal of a small school provided a home and car when I first started. When I was sick she cared for me. When she retired she became a valuable assistant when I averaged three programs a day with much travel. After establishing an enviable reputation I could offer a block of time to a city and the Superintendent would send me through all his schools and I was earning over $200 a week. Vacation times were spent making movies of wild life, Indian lore and entertaining children's camps and cruises on the Great Lakes.

Filming the Myan pyramids and ancient ruins of the great civilization in Yucatan, living with people of an extremely different culture, gave us another program. While there Miss Vincent fell in love with a baby monkey who adopted her as a mother. When Hermie added three trained dogs to her family we had to have trailer that we named "Bitazoo". The children loved her little show but their care hindered the "Bird Hike" program. That winter as we headed south we were robbed in Knoxville. Programs had to be canceled. I took a job as a guide in a State Park and then the restrictions of the war make travel impossible.

God was closing the door of self effort in order to open up a whole new life that was far beyond anything I could ask or think. I pray that the brief account of the adventures of His bond servant will encourage many to surrender to the Lord Jesus Christ.

(R to L) Miss Vincent, Juanita and Tetna— a black spider monkey from Yucatan.

CHAPTER 1

❦

Actually Believing Christ

From a human perspective, I had made it to the top as an educational entertainer; the future seemed even more exciting—then robbers stole our equipment.

Soon war was declared, gas and tires were restricted, and I became a guide and photographer for a state park in Florida.

A ranger progressed from a mutual friend to a lover. The aging, retired school teacher who had been my assistant for several years became very depressed. Her teacher's pension paid only $300.00 a year; I had been her support. Fear of losing that security drove her to thoughts of suicide.

Since she had helped me when I first started my programs by nursing me through an operation, providing a home for my headquarters, and a car, and, after her retirement, traveling over dangerous roads to get me to my heavy schedule, I felt it was my duty to break off the hope of marriage and a nice home in order to care for her through her derangement.

We were given a seventeen-acre farm and orchard near St. Cloud, Florida, rent-free for taking care of it. I began teaching in the high school. I was teaching subjects I hadn't seen since I was in high school. Also, there were warring factions among the students, and the principal was afraid to do anything to discipline the students. It was a nightmare. Besides the load of teaching, was the fear that the one at home would destroy herself in her derangement.

Where she had loved children, now she had no interest in anything except her monkey, three trained dogs and the stock—chickens, ducks, rabbits and pigs.

With the heavy load of chores and school responsibilities, I was getting no more than four hours in bed. By mid-semester, I was totally exhausted; God had brought me to the end of my ability to cope with the situation.

It was at this time that the Lord sent a young man from a Baptist seminary to speak to the student body for only ten minutes.

"You are all looking for happiness," he stated.

I said to myself, Yes, and I sure missed the boat.

He continued, "Real happiness is found in the word joy: J stands for Jesus, O stands for others, and Y stands for you; that is the key that opens the door to the happiness you are seeking. If you want real joy, let Jesus come into your heart. He'll wash away your sins and replace your dark times with real and lasting joy. If Jesus is not Lord of all, He is not Lord at all."

In those few moments, he explained how sin made us selfish and pride made us want to be first. That was the way down into darkness. Only as we put Jesus Christ as Lord of all, and others before ourselves, would we be able to open the door to new and eternal joy.

I could think of nothing the rest of the day except what that fine young man had said.

After the chores were done at 11 o'clock that night, I took one weary step after another out into the moonlit orchard and fell on my face before a mighty God who was waiting.

All the churches I had faithfully attended had never taught that Jesus must be, Lord of all my heart. I had accepted Jesus as my Savior in evangelistic meetings, was baptized and joined a church. I felt called to become a missionary at that time, and was zealous in my attempt to win others to the Savior, and to lead a Christian life. I was taught the stories of the Bible heroes, but not their application to life here and now.

Through my university and a teachers' college, churches taught that the Bible contained the Word of God—but there were many errors. They took out what they liked; the rest were just allegories and fables that were supposed to teach a lesson. By the time they told us what wasn't true, there was no time to get the so-called lesson. About all they left of the Bible was the cover.

If the Bible isn't true, what is the use of going to church?

The hypocrisy I saw in the leaders disgusted me. I decided I'd just try to lead a moral life the best I could. If they couldn't see Jesus as my Savior by my walk, what was the use of my talk?

When I was prostrate before the holy God that night, there was no visable form; but by comparing my self-righteousness and His perfection, I was conscious for the first time of my own total depravity. It seemed that the burden of my sin would crush me. I cried for mercy. The miracle of His precious blood cleansing me thoroughly went through me.

Joy flooded my soul. It seemed the mighty, tender hand of my Savior reached down to His worn-out child to lift me up. All the physical tiredness was gone. I felt His life flowing through me. If I could fly I'd have taken off.

"Oh God," I thrilled, "this is the most wonderful thing that has ever happened to me. I don't want it to ever end. From now on, you're the boss. I want you to be the Lord of all. From now on, you lead me. I'll go where you want me to go, be what you want me to be, and do what you want me to do."

It was then I felt the call again to become a missionary, as He had called me when I had accepted Him as my Savior at sixteen.

With renewed strength, I returned to the same exterior burdens; but there was a new love, a new purpose, and His strength. The Word of God became exciting; hymns I'd sung for years, now had far deeper meaning. At times, tears would flow as they spoke to my heart.

On Saturdays, I would deliver the farm produce to customers. What didn't sell, I took to the pastor's family of the church we attended—where my friend would go. If I went without her, she would be depressed for days. The pastor looked like a saint, with white, wavy hair and a pleasing personality.

One day when my friend had gone to visit her sisters, this pastor came unexpectedly to make a pastoral call. I was in my work clothes and busy. I didn't even invite him to sit down. Standing in the middle of the living room, he began asking me personal questions. I told him I'd broken up with the man I thought of marrying because of my friend's threat to destroy herself.

Suddenly he attacked me, trying to throw me onto the davenport. I was shocked. "No, no, don't try anything like that. I want to think of you as a man of God."

"I wasn't going to hurt you," he replied." I just wanted to see if you were normal."

"If that's being normal, I'm not that kind. Please leave and never return." I never returned to his church. I felt I was in a trap.

How I longed for freedom to live my own life, but if I left and the friend ended her life in her derangement I would feel her blood was on my shoulders. "In your way and your time," I prayed, "you will lead me on. If you do it, you will be responsible for her life."

CHAPTER 2

Adventures Become Common

A year after my Lord revealed Himself to me, He spoke again as clearly as He had that night out in the orchard, "Now I want you to go into the military."

"Oh no, Lord," I pleaded, "anywhere but there." I remembered my promise to go where He wanted me to go. "But Lord, you know many of those girls drink, and I would get sick if I had to live in a stinky room full of cigarette smoke. They're just not my kind of girls; some are immoral, and I'd be classed with them."

"You think you are better than the worst of them?" He chided. "But for my grace, you would be the same. I'm sending you to be a missionary to the military. Will you obey?"

"All right, Lord, I yield. I'll go wherever you want me to go." I had fought the Lord for a month and hadn't gotten anywhere. The moment I submitted to His directive will, the joy returned.

Not explaining my reasons for going to Jacksonville, I went to the recruiting office for the WAVES (Women Appointed for Voluntary Emergency Service). From 8:00 a.m. until 4:00 p.m., I filled out their questionnaires, waited and had more interviews until the time to be sworn in. As I stood before an officer, a little voice inside said, No.

"Pardon me," I spoke to the lieutenant, "before I'm sworn in I'd like to see what the SPARS (Semper Paratus—always ready) have to offer."

"Oh no, you don't want to do that," she crooned. "Just sign on this line and you'll be through."

The more she coerced, the more sure I was that I wasn't where God wanted me.

"I haven't signed on the dotted line yet," smilingly but determined, "and you can't make me."

Dejected, "I guess I can't."

"Then, may I please be excused?"

"I guess I'll have to let you."

I walked over to the SPAR office. As I put my hand on the door knob, that voice said, This is it.

Inside, I was greeted as a person—not just a number.

"What department are you interested in?"

"Photography." The Lord had told me.

"Isn't that a coincidence." The young lady held up a letter. "It just came from Coast Guard HQ asking us to enlist more photographers."

Another assurance of His leading.

I had arrived at 4:30. The girls stayed overtime to process me and, by 6:30, I was a SPAR instead of a WAVE. I was not just a number. They treated me as an important person—called me by my name.

"How soon can you go to boot camp?"

"The sooner the better," I responded. "It will be like a morgue when I get home."

"The next training starts in ten days."

"That's going to be hard, but I'll try to make it." In another month, I'd be beyond the age limit.

I returned to the little farm and explained to my aging partner, "When you retired and got only $300.00 a year, I needed an assistant to help drive, set up stage scenery and be a companion. I told you there were good times with plenty, other times with no income, but I had never gone hungry. If you wanted to help me, I promised you would never go hungry.

Now I want to be free to serve my Lord and my country. All I want now is a $10.00 bill and the clothes on my back. You may have the rest."

I took her to St. Petersburg to be near her sisters. The sale of our stock and equipment bought an acreage and a nice little house. She got a job in the Veterans Hospital, where she worked for men who suffered more than she ever had as the daughter of an alcoholic. She lived into her eighties, well-fixed. I was free at last, praising the Lord.

The trainload of girls unloaded at Palm Beach, Florida. We passed the check-in desk in single file. Six girls to each room in this big resort hotel. Room 506 included me. Of the 5000 in the hotel, I think I was with the nicest girls. Only one smoked and she had friends elsewhere, so I slept in a smokeless room—God's arrangement.

As we waited in line for meals or orders and girls were bored from waiting, I would joke and lead in some of the fun choruses, treating it all as a game. When waiting in long lines for meals, I'd begin whistling like a canary, and the complaining stopped as they listened.

We had classes every other day and work duty the other. My job was washing trays in a disinfectant tub then stacking them in racks to push them through the steaming washer.

My garment ran streams of steam and sweat eight hours a day—with time out to eat, shower and get back to sweat some more.

"How can you be so happy," the girls would ask, "when you have such a miserable job?"

"It isn't what your hands are doing that makes you happy, it's what your heart is doing. It's the love of the Lord that brings joy."

Girls along the line would slip out for an extra rest as soon as the officer left. Finally, I'd be alone finishing up jobs neglected by others, so I'd not leave until all was shipshape. As far as I knew, only the Lord saw me. I did it for Him.

One day before graduation, the Captain came for inspection. He felt my dripping garment and exploded, "You can't do this to any of our girls! This is inhuman! If this condition is not corrected immediately, some of you in charge will be demoted—period."

Air conditioning was installed after I left. I had been in Florida six winters and three summers, so I was acclimated and didn't faint like some did from the heat.

Each SPAR was personally interviewed to see where they could best serve their country. It was my turn. A kindly officer interrogated, "You're a jack of all trades. You could fit into any number of positions. What do you want me to put down as first choice?"

"Photography."

"What laboratory experience have you had?"

"None. I've never even seen inside a photo lab, but I'd like to learn. I've taken good pictures, slides and thousands of feet of color motion pictures used in our programs. I graduated in fine arts and know good composition."

"But what they need is laboratory technicians. The men do most of the photography. We are a small branch and have no schools like the navy, so that lets you out of photography. What's your next choice?"

"Photography."

"Since you insist, I'll put that down as first choice, but you won't get it. You'll get your second or third choice."

"That's OK. Whatever my country chooses for me to do, I'll give it my best."

One of my friends worked in the office where interviews were processed. "I got your papers today," she revealed. "That is the best report I've ever read." I was encouraged.

A couple of the girls had been causing the whole unit to be restricted from leave because of their disregard for the rules. We were to meet at a new place for marching. As usual, I was late getting off work so the girls were gone. I asked our company commander where it was. "I'm on my way there now. I'll take you."

As we walked along she said, "I'm not going to ask you who the girls are who are messing around, but I'll tell you...." She named the two girls. I didn't say anything.

After the parade, I returned to my room. As I walked, the corridor girls who had been friendly turned away. I felt icicles forming. "What's going on here?" I asked my roommates.

"You squealed on those girls to an officer, and that just isn't done. They saw you with an officer and right after the parade, they were called on the carpet."

"But I didn't tell her anything. I asked her for directions and she said she'd take me. You don't refuse to walk with an officer, do you? I can't go up and down the hall and insist I didn't squeal on them, but I can live and love so much that they won't believe what they heard."

At graduation, I was looking lovingly at the two girls who had caused the misunderstanding; friendships were re-established.

🦜 🦜 🦜

Assignments were announced, "Juanita McComb: photography...."

I was elated. They'll put me in some little lab, but I can work up, I thought.

"...You are to report to HQ in Washington DC."

Wow! They had the reputation for the finest photography in the world.

An entire train loaded with SPAR graduates rolled into the station at 2 a.m.; busses filled as names were called. Hour after hour, they rolled away to hotels—requisitioned until Coast Guard barracks could be built for the SPARS. Standing alone at dawn as the last bus moved off, my name was called, "McComb, report to this address."

I took a streetcar, located a three-story, brick residence in a nice neighborhood. A white-haired, motherly lady invited me to a cheery, third-floor room with three beds. She sat on one.

"It's been a long time since we got a new girl in this home. Do you know why you were selected to come here?"

"No, but I'm interested."

"This is an honor home. Only those who have a perfect record get to live here. No officer is in charge. You are on your own."

I reported to Coast Guard HQ on Pennsylvania Avenue. A middle-aged lieutenant warmly welcomed me, "Do you know why I requested for you to come to HQ?" he asked.

"No, but I'm interested."

"You obey orders to the letter. We get experienced technicians who come wanting to do it their way. I chose you because I want to train you in every department to do it my way."

That he did. Again, the Lord chose my roommates and most of those in the home didn't smoke.

I started attending the big-city church of the same denomination as my parents, hoping to make closer ties with them. I was made to feel important. Soon, the pastor took me aside and asked me to get my folks to send more money to the national church. The minister of music told the large group of young adults that a lot of the old fashioned songs should be eliminated, "Stately songs, like 'Holy, Holy, Holy,' are OK, but songs like 'What Can Wash Away My Sins' and 'Nothing But the Blood of Jesus' have no place in our music. That's butcherhouse religion. Who of us have ever sinned?" he concluded.

"I have." I was shocked. "His blood shed for me is my life." I walked out. Shopping for a church where He was loved and the Word was taught was unrewarded.

Then a girl invited me to go to a mission hall with her. She seemed so wholesome, I consented. I'll try anything once, I reasoned.

As a child, I'd been invited to a holy-roller mission and escaped when they went into their emotional hysteria.But this mission was the Rescue Mission near by.

As we opened the door, I felt the Spirit of God telling me, This is it. The Navigators were using the mission auditorium on Saturday evenings and Sunday mornings. At last, I had found brothers and sisters in Christ who loved the Lord as I did.

After the morning service, the men went to a home led by Lt. James Downing and the women to another home—where his wife, Morena, and her mother welcomed us, fed us and made us feel loved. After a rest, we gathered in the back yard for prayer. Then, in teams, they went to churches to help with special music, etc. For the first time, I was introduced to a fundamental evangelical church. They ministered to me. The "liberal churches" were after all they could get from me and cared nothing for my real soul's need.

A telegram reached me at the lab: My father had passed away. It had been four years since I'd seen my dear mother. I was eligible for a two-week leave, so I wondered how I could get there for the funeral. At the Rescue Mission, quite a number of children had been taken there when parents had paid their way into a movie and disappeared. At midnight, the children were turned out onto the street with no place to go except into the caring arms of Christians who would be there to take them to the mission. All I could spare went to help feed them and show love to those needy kids.

I had no money left; how could I go? My personnel officer said, "We'll lend you the money and make reservations on the train for you. Payment will be taken out of your check a little at a time, so it'll be no problem."

"But I've always made it a principle in my life never to charge or to borrow. Can't I fly on one of the transport planes like the men do?"

"We are a smaller unit. We've never been able to get a flight for one of our SPARS on a navy or army plane."

"Is there any law against trying?"

"No, but you won't get it, so I'll loan you the fare and reserve a place on the train."

Assured the Lord was leading, I went to the airport. They gave me a ride to Kansas City. As I asked for another ride, a pilot stepped up and offered to take me with them to Midland, Texas.

"We're flying, dead reckoning," the pilot told me. "We need to repair a brake pedal here. If we get it fixed so we can land in Long Beach in daylight, you can go that far." It was too late by the time they were ready to fly so they took me out to eat and put me up in an unused officers' home.

At daylight, we lifted off. One of the men was playing with a dog while we waited. In the scuffle, his blue pants got a tear from sharp toenails. I had him change while I mended the pants. The rest of our flight, I was sewing on buttons, etc., for the men—we had become friends.

Landing in Long Beach, a jeep pulled alongside, "Want a ride to the gate?" We all climbed in.

Another car met us at the gate, "Want a ride into LA?" We all climbed in. They let me out at the bus depot.

I was just in time to catch the bus to Temple City. It had cost me thirty-five cents to get home. My little nephew ran up the street to welcome me. My love went out to him.

My younger sister had chosen the way of the world. My heart ached for her two sons who had been moved back and forth between my parents, the military academy, an occasional stay with their mother, and one of their step-fathers.

Mother was so glad to see me. We got little sleep as she unloaded her trials related to my sister and her husbands and children. My father's sister came and I had to sleep with her. She snored all night, talked all day and wanted to see all the sights around LA while she was there. So by leaving time, I was tired out.

"Aren't you going to take the train back?" they asked.

"No, the Lord brought me out, and I believe He'll take me back."

My sister worked in the shipyards in Long Beach right across from the airport where I came in.

"There's nothing going out today, but you may stay in the barracks and we'll let you know if something comes along."

Next morning they said there was a flight going east out of Burbank, so they took me 65 miles north to get me back to Washington DC.

Over Cleveland, the plane suddenly made a nose dive through the clouds. Fear shone on the faces of the passengers. Pulling out beneath the dark shroud, the plane banked sharply, but landed safely.

It was soon to take off again for New York. Three passengers had to give over their seats to higher-ranking officers. They didn't pass the straws to me. One man drew the short straw, and it looked like he would burst into tears.

"Does it mean a lot to you to go on this flight?" I asked.

"If I don't get that plane, I'll have to go overseas without seeing my mother."

"You take my place. I have a little time to get to my station." He brightened.

In the morning, I got a flight right into Washington DC. I had one hour to change and go on duty. God answers prayer: He gave me the trip; it only cost ten cents to get back.

"You were just lucky," they tried to say. Another girl in our lab figured if I could, she could, too. She was a beautiful girl. She got a ride, but the plane crashed. She wasn't hurt badly, but she wasn't under the protective hand of the Lord.

Later on, I got word that the people who moved onto the farm in Florida had gone and left it empty. Natives feel an empty place is up for grabs. The trunk with my stage scenery and silk paintings of birds was in the attic. No one would go to rescue them for me.

"May I go to Florida on a 5-day leave I have coming?" I asked.

"You can't get to Florida and back in five days."

"I hoped I could fly."

"Well," she smiled, "I know what you've been doing for these girls and I trust you implicitly. So when you get there, if you need a couple of extra days, you phone me and I'll fix it up for you."

My leave started at midnight. I took the streetcar to the air base. "There's a flight going to Florida at 9 o'clock in the morning." I rested in the waiting room and reported.

"Do you have a priority?" she asked.

"Not the kind you're talking about," I said smiling.

"I'm sorry, but this is strictly a priority plane, so I can't put you on. But if you stick around, I'll fix it up."

Half an hour later, "Juanita McComb, your plane is waiting for you."

I was escorted to the private plane of the commander-in-chief of the armed forces of America. I sat in all the comforts of his overstuffed seat. Windows replaced the gun turrets used over enemy territory, so I enjoyed beautiful cloud formations. High-ranking officers were controlling the swiftest plane of that day. I was given a passenger report sheet every little while by a sharp, young pilot.

"You treat me just like the commander," I marveled.

"We consider you as just as important as the chief." He bowed. In no time at all, we were in Palm Beach. I checked in and asked if there were any flights to Fort Myers.

"None go across the peninsula, but go down to Miami and up the west coast." One of the pilots who had been on my flight was asking for a ride to Miami.

"Is there room for one more?" I asked the pilot. He took a good look at me.

"If I siphon out enough gas to counteract your weight and baggage, I can put you on."

"Oh, that would be too much trouble."

"That's OK. Get your slacks on. Do you have a parachute?"

"No."

"I'll get you one." He fitted it on me. In half an hour, we were in Miami. I called some old friends; they were thrilled.

"The room we rented out was just left empty, and it's all clean and ready for you." After a delightful visit, I decided to take a bus to Fort Myers to make it easier for my friends to send me on my way.

As the line filed into the bus, a chain was drawn across in front of me. "Now all the seats are full. If you want to stand, you can get on." I thought I could sit on my suitcase, so I climbed in.

The people in the back seat had their heads together. They motioned to me, "We felt if we squeezed closer together you could sit with us." Through the hot, hot ride we became friends. They were dear people. They enjoyed my stories.

Leonard was waiting for me. I had told him I was coming, but I didn't know how. He had met every train, plane and bus; and, at last, he found me. The years I was caring for my partner, I cut off all connection with him, but letters renewed our communication after I was in the service.

He took me for a beautiful ride in his yacht before taking me to the farm. It was sad to see how everything that could be stolen was gone. I went into the attic. The radio and other things were gone, but the old trunk with the old farm clothes on top of my silk paintings—carefully rolled in plastic and a black covering—hadn't been discovered down in the bottom. Praise the Lord!

As we drove toward St. Petersburg, I asked Leonard what he thought of Jesus.

"You don't expect me to believe in that old supernatural stuff that he was God do you?"

"Why, yes, don't you?"

"No. He was a great man...ahead of his time...idealistic and nice ethics, but the Son of God? No, I have too much education to believe that."

"Why do you go to church, then?"

"It's a nice, cultural thing to do. It's quieting to my nerves and has nice music, but I pay no attention to the sermons. No...He was just a man."

When we were dating, Leonard and I seemed to match interests well. We were the same age and were educated in common interests, like nature, art and photography.

Now, since I had met the Lord Jesus Christ, I was on an opposite course.He could not see into the spiritual dimensions that had become my very life. No amount of evidence of the miracles in the Bible, or in modern life, would convince him.

We visited my former partner and went on to Tampa, to the base. I had tried bus and train passages. Standing room only had been overbooked. President F. D. Roosevelt was dead; all planes were grounded. I called my officer and she gave me two extra days. I was welcomed to stay in the girls' barracks. Not seeing them, I inquired and found I'd gone beyond a block south of the row. As I came past the last building, a young lady was on the porch and called, "Are you looking for a place to stay tonight?"

"Yes." A spacious lawn separated us.

"Come in and stay with me. I have an empty bed. I'll fix it up with the OD"

I turned in. The big, bare barn of a room contained two-layer bunk beds. I sat on the lower bunk, she saw how tired I looked and left me to sleep. In honor of the president's death, soft music was sent out over the intercom. I fell asleep. As I enjoyed a refreshing shower, a voice in the next stall said, "You're a Christian, aren't you!"

"Yes, are you?" I called back to the voice.

"Yes, that's why I invited you to come into my barracks. I'm the head of this one with sixty-five girls, and I'm the only Christian.

That evening, in her private room, I felt at home with a true sister-in-Christ. We shared the wonders of His grace. On our knees, we fellowshipped in praise and prayer.

As we enjoyed breakfast together, my name was called over the intercom. A lieutenant commander had been ordered to Charlotte, North Carolina; he invited me to go along. They had told me all planes had been grounded and there was no way I could get a flight. But God doesn't pay any attention to the impossibilities.

As the pilots took us north, the commander told of interesting things, but soon he was listening to my stories of new life for all who trust in the Savior. As we parted, he thanked me for sharing my testimony with him. The Lord got me on a train the rest of the way. Again, I had one hour to get changed and be on duty.

Fine, new barracks were built for us right behind the Smithsonian Institution. We could walk back and forth to HQ. Again, I had no choice of a roommate, but God gave me a clean-cut, young girl who didn't smoke and who worked with me in the lab. I was like a mom to her.

CHAPTER 3

Apply Biblical Christianity
WITNESS AT WORK

A new girl came to our lab. We all went to lunch as a happy cluster and invited Earnie to join us, but she avoided us every time.

"Well, if she's going to be stuck up and not be friendly, we'll let her alone."

"No, girls, I can tell she has heart trouble and needs a friend. You go on. I'll read till she comes out and I'll join her."

It worked. When she felt alone, she started to the mess hall and I fell in step with her. As I befriended her, I learned of the terrible home she was running away from. She was under the age limit and so afraid she'd be sent back to her worthless father. I took her under my wing and the hurt and fear began to disappear. We used to take little girls who had been forsaken by their parents on outings, and the rosebud would begin to open. She had the skill of an artist and did well in the lab, but finally it was discovered that her birth certificate was forged so she was up for dishonorable discharge. l went to bat for her and told why she had escaped a miserable life; so she was given an honorable discharge.

On the train, she met a soldier who knew suffering, too. After their marriage, she wrote, "At last, I'm really loved and wanted. She was now a Christian and Jesus loved her, too.

"What are you up to now?" old friends were writing. "The Secret Service has been tracing your history all the way back through high school."

My lieutenant approached me, "Would you be willing to take specialized training with the navy for a top-secret position in New York City? The officer in charge now is needed overseas, and you are the only one in the Coast Guard who is eligible to replace him."

So, I was introduced into the new photographic capabilities of the Naval Air Photography—trained, treated as an officer and, when I'd finished the course, I returned.

"Do you think you could handle the job?" my boss asked.

"I think I could, but I don't feel that is the type of work the Lord is leading me into."

After discussing the feeling with a higher officer, they asked if I would be willing to go to Alaska to start a photo lab for them up there. I said I'd always wanted to go to Alaska and would go if my petty officer rate that was overdue was given to me first. Just then, I came down with bronchitis and went to sick bay.

The girls in the lab came to visit me, "Hurry up and get well. The fellows don't treat us the same when you're not there."

In all these months, I never heard a swear word or dirty story. Men who developed and printed pictures of beach landings on the islands of the Pacific would come into the privacy of my lab for a cup of coffee and a heart-to-heart talk about what to expect if they were among the bodies strewn along the beaches of Saipan, Palau and Guam. If they didn't return, I hoped their next flight was upward.

When I returned to my lab, one of the girls informed me my name wasn't on the list for petty officer, and it was supposed to be. I checked with my boss. He was sure it was, but it had slipped out of the list seemingly by accident. So the draft of girls went to Alaska without me. At that time, bombs were dropping on Hiroshima and Nagasaki and all rates were frozen.

🐦 🐦 🐦

Another turn of events was a month in the galley. All SPARS were required to take one month work there, but my boss said I was indispensable. I had been there over a year, so the higher-ups insisted I serve one month on my second year. I didn't mind. I had plenty of experience having worked my way through the university.

The boss of the dining and kitchen area was lower in rank, but over me in the job. In between the rush hours, we would all take out reading material and rest. One day the boss came near. "From the look on your face you must be reading something real interesting."

"I am," I replied. "It's the greatest love story in all the world." The cover title was: The Greatest Love Story.

She grabbed the Gospel of John out of my hand, gazed in amazement and recognized it as part of the Bible, "You take that to your room and never bring it back."

At closing, with all there to receive instruction or criticism, she bawled me out angrily for reading while on duty.

"You don't have to take her lip," the girls were defensive. "Report her. We can read anything we please while we rest. You have the same right."

"Don't you touch her! She has heart trouble." After that, she was mean to me—giving me the hardest jobs—but I took it with a smile.

One day, I had to stack cases of glass milk bottles. They were heavy. I was swinging the last case onto the stack above my head in the walk-in cooler, when my wrist twisted. Pain and a black-and-blue arm sent me to the doctor. He put on splints and ace bandages, and sent a notice that I was to be given only light work.

The boss insisted I was faking it to get out of work, so she gave me the heaviest jobs she could. I did it—pain or no pain— and replaced the soaked bandages when through.

The day my month ended, all the crew had gone. I was alone with my boss. She came close, "Would you pray for me?" I could see the tears in her eyes. "I'm in deep trouble."

She continued to unload a heart that had reached the end of her endurance. It was worth all my pain; God had sent me. When I passed her testing, she could trust me with her problems.

Another incident I'll never forget was my letter to Leonard. We had kept up our writing. I sent books to read and all kinds of evidence to prove Jesus is God. One day the Holy Spirit seemed to be using my hand to present my faith in a logical and convincing flow of facts. It became several pages, so my friend, who was the chaplain's assistant, promised to type it for me. When I went in, she wasn't there, but a Jewess who assisted the Jewish chaplain offered to type it for me. As she began, the rapid clicking of the keys slowed to a stop. She looked up. In a hushed voice, "This is the strangest letter I've ever read."

I began to explain my reason for writing it. Just as I began to explain my faith, another Jewess came in and heard me say, "I believe…"

This new arrival, clenching her fist and teeth, spit out, "I could tell you in three words what I believe!"

"What do you believe?"

Like an explosion, "I believe nothing!!

As I was looking up at her with a love from my Lord, the words began to flow. I told her the love of God was so great that He sent His only Son to become a man—born of a Jewish virgin—to live a perfect life in spite of all the suffering and rejection, in order that He could die in our place so that God's holy law was satisfied.

I explained that all sin must be paid for, "The wages of sin is death." All have sinned and come short of the glory of God so all deserve death, but because Jesus had no sin He was able to take the death penalty for us. He satisfied the law and, after three days, He arose from the grave.

For forty days he appeared to many of those who had put their trust in Him. While 500 stood on the Mount of Olives, He gave them His last instructions. While all watched in awe, the Shekina Glory cloud lifted Him skyward. After He disappeared, angels told the crowd that some day He would come again in the same way, to the same place. When He comes, every Jewish soul will believe in the Messiah when He comes as King of Kings and Lord of Lords.

As if in a daze, the young Jewess walked over to the window. We remained silent while she was in deep thought. Slowly, she turned and walked out the door.

"That was just what she needed," the typist marveled.

As far as I know Leonard never yielded to the Savior, but that letter opened the hearts of two, young, Jewish ladies. That was one of God's appointments: One plants, another waters— but God gives the increase.

After I removed the rose-colored glasses and saw the proud self-centered man that Leonard really was, I continually thanked the Lord that I hadn't married him.

I would have been boxed into pleasing one man. I determined to never take one step toward marriage again. God had such wonderful adventures in His plan that I could have never dreamed of just up the highway.

The last weeks of the war were unpredictable in HQ. The promised rate and trip to Alaska were delayed. Then, the very day they came through, peace was declared. The world went wild in celebration, but we who loved the Lord went to church to worship and praise Him.

CHAPTER 4

Adaptability By Choice
ON TO CALIFORNIA

That night, I learned I was eligible for discharge. I had a choice of going to Alaska, staying at HQ or getting discharged.

Every Thursday we women gathered at the girls' Navigator home for Bible study. Never had I heard such wonderful explanations from the Word that applied to our life.

If I could learn to understand and teach God's Word like Morena, I'd be the happiest girl on earth, I thought.

As I started proceedings for discharge, I wasn't expecting to get the GI Bill for more education; when I enlisted, only those under thirty were eligible. So I thought of the contract still waiting to be signed to give my Bird Hike program in the schools on the west side of the Rockies. I could be making $200 a week. If I saved, I could go to Bible school the next year.

As I was proceeding, someone asked if I was going to apply for the GI Bill? I said I was too old.

"No," I was told, "anyone can have one year."

"Wonderful, I'll go for it!"

I called Morena. She was gone.

"I want to go to Bible school where Morena went." Her mother told me she went to Biola. I thought she said *Viola*. I rushed over to the Library of Congress, but found no Bible school called *Viola*. I didn't care if it was just a little hole in the wall; if they could teach me to teach the Word like she does, I'd go there. Thursday's Bible study cleared the mistake. Biola means Bible Institute of Los Angeles.

"But there's a long waiting list to get in," Morena warned. "It would take a miracle if you were accepted at this late date. But I'll try."

Saturday fellowship turned into a farewell party for me, and a beautiful leather Schofield Bible was given. The leader was announcing how I planned to go to Bible school as soon as I could raise the funds. Morena came in waving a telegram...I had been accepted. Celebration!

But now it would take another miracle to get me discharged in time for the September semester. The dear officer who had given me extra days when I went to Florida went to work to get me out. Then bad news: There had to be so many girls at a time to go through the process. I was the only one in DC who was eligible. She said she'd pull every string in her power to help me. She routed girls from all over to come through DC to pick me up and get me out in time. Discharging SPARS was a new experience. So much time was wasted. One would say it was impossible to clear before Labor Day. The next would say they'd try. Just at 6 o'clock—after a hectic day—we were given a speech of appreciation, the National Anthem, and the popular song "Time on Your Hands."

We all dashed for the ferry—jammed in so tight we had to hold our suitcases on our heads. Then we ran for the train. I was last, so I had to sit on a bench. It turned out to be a little milk train that stopped at every little town. The air conditioning wouldn't work. The conductor refused to open doors and windows hoping it would start, but we were suffocating. So, in desperation, they opened them up and the black smoke settled on our sweat-drenched bodies. We were all pretty black by the time we reached our station.

🐦 🐦 🐦

To make up for lost time, I flew to Orlando and then on to Tampa—to the airport where I'd been given rides before. This time, I was a veteran with no priority. A lieutenant offered me a ride as far as he was going. He outfitted me with a parachute and instructions on what to pull if I needed it. We boarded an old bomber that had just returned from Germany. It looked like a patchwork quilt. It had been filled with holes on its many flights over targets.

A few men climbed in with me. The pilot said, "If you hear this signal you are to bail out. Understand? If you don't, you'll be flying in this crate all by yourself."

Our first stop, we safely landed and the lieutenant took me out to breakfast. "How do you ever remember what to push and what to pull with all those gadgets on the cockpit panels?" I queried.

"Would you like to watch me fly it?"

"Oh, would they let me?"

"You can if you wait till we get out of sight of the airport."

When safely airborne, the copilot came after me. My parachute had to be removed in order to walk the narrow board through the huge belly of the ship. The bomb bay was empty now. The double doors that opened way below me would no longer drop death from its big mouth. I held onto guy wires as I carefully walked the plank. The lieutenant said it wouldn't be too exciting for a while, so I could crawl up overhead and sit in the nose gunner's position.

There I sat—machine guns in all directions—in a big plastic bubble. I could see everywhere except behind. To give me some extra thrills, he swooped down over farms and up through rain clouds. Then it was time to watch the men land the big old bird. From the time they called in, it took both men talking to the airport while working both hands as fast as they could until we were safely on the runway.

I thanked the friendly pilots and said good-bye. When I checked to see if any other flights were going west, a captain

stepped up and said I could go with him. He was headed for
Cheyenne and Salt Lake City, if he could get planes that far. The
first hop was to Oklahoma City. The men flying with us waited
to see if the captain would get another plane out. I reported at
the desk, but they told me this was strictly a priority airport.

"I guess I've been bumped here," I told the men.

"Now you wait till the captain returns. You know he said we
could ride with him if he got a hop." Just then, the captain came
striding along motioning for us to follow. We did. In moments,
we were zooming over the city and on our way to Wyoming.

The captain had been a test pilot with many daring thrillers
to share. He put the plane in remote control so he could come
back with us and tell stories of his narrow escapes. As we
neared the mountains, he took over. Air pockets made a rough
ride at times; those planes were not built for comfort. Hard
seats of pressed wood against the sides have a hump for each
rump. No way can you stretch out to rest. So I always carried a
little pillow with me.

A black man was so tired, he slept in such a painful
position, I slipped my pillow under his head as he slept. When
he awoke, he saw what I'd done and came over.

"Y'all sho' must be a Christian, ma'am."

"I am, are you?"

"Yes ma'am!" emphatically.

He sat beside me and over the mountains we enjoyed sweet
fellowship.

Landing in Cheyenne, our captain said he had a date in Salt
Lake City if he hurried. We got out of one plane. He ran in and
ran out again. We ran to another with him, and we shot into the
sky. When we braked to a halt in Salt Lake, she was waiting for
him.

The men and I checked in. I turned to my black friend, "I
guess I'll have to go on from here by bus. This is a priority
airport."

"Now, ma'am, y'all been a good friend to me. I's been
travelin' on these planes a lot. I know three men got off that
plane I's goin on, and I's the only one waitin' to git on, so I

knows they's plenty o' room for you. When my plane is called, you follow me." He picked up my suitcase and we climbed on. The pilots walked to the cockpit, shut the door, and we were off.

"Now, ma'am, they won't put you off now," jubilantly. "An' the nex' stop is Sac-re-mento."

Another man spent most of his time reading his Bible. Another friend who loved the Lord was on leave to meet his newborn son. We felt well acquainted after our long trip through the skies.

Landing, a jeep pulled up to take us into town. My Christian friends planned to catch rides to LA if they could, and offered to take me with them. Being very short of money I felt it was OK. Out of town, we waited in separate spots. I was with the young father. Soon we were given rides as far as Bakersfield. It was getting to be afternoon, so I told my friend I'd take a bus on in, for I didn't want to be caught after dark. He took the bus with me.

I got into the LA bus depot in the middle of the night. It was out of the question to try to go on to Temple City—Mother's home. So I asked the matron in the restrooms to protect me if I fell asleep, for I was very tired. The night sights in the restroom—women who were beaten trying to escape a drunken master, prostitutes, slaves of the under world—I'll never forget. I prayed for those souls for whom Christ died. No one had cared for their souls and given them the good news. Perhaps they, too, could be saved.

At dawn, I went by streetcar to Biola. It was the very last day I could register for that semester. The hundred dollars I received from the military discharge was enough to meet my immediate needs until the GI Bill came through. After a full day of classes, I went to my mother's home in Temple City. She had so much to tell me that I had another night with almost no sleep. "As thy day so shall thy strength be." How often I've claimed that promise.

CHAPTER 5

Attending Bible College
MY FAITH WALK AT BIOLA

Mother needed me so much that I commuted that year. My sister, her sons and present husband were imposing on her—breaking her heart as they went after the sinful things of the world.

My load was extra hard. Most of the students had been in Bible-teaching churches. Here, I was taking seminary courses and had to memorize hundreds of verses and facts new to me. Then, I was late starting and had to make up what I missed. I got little rest at Mother's home as I met her needs.

Yet the Lord was with me. I was excited in all I was learning. The students were so kind and thoughtful of others; such a contrast to those in the military where most were looking out for number one.

And the professors! They were devoted friends! Not high-and-mighty acting like the profs I'd had at the university. I loved every one there.

That summer, Mother flew to Lincoln to visit my older sister. While she was gone, my younger sister threw a wild party and the landlord kicked them out. They rented a little old house, took all they wanted of Mother's things, and put the rest and a cot for her out on a screened porch. So I arranged for her to stay with friends, and I moved into the dorm in a single room. Greek was hard for me, and I needed much time to study.

A call for workers for vacation Bible school teachers with the Lockman Foundation to reach the suburbs, found around thirty girls ready to live in tents in a Eucalyptus grove and go in teams to the villages. I was the special feature, going the rounds each week with my object lessons, bird songs and stories. We had a robed choir that sang many places and Mr. Lockman gave his testimony. Joy Ridderhof of Gospel Recordings spoke a couple of times at our evening campfires.

Her faith walk was used of the Lord to help me trust Him in the years to come when I launched out into the deep.

As a reward, Mr. Lockman chartered a boat and took us to Catalina Island for a thrilling view of God's underwater garden.

Near the end of my second year, Mr. Grey called for volunteers to lead VBS in the foothills and mountains of northern California. After I offered to go, other students warned, "You don't want to go out under that mission. He gets you out in some wild place in the middle of summer and runs out of money, so he sends you home at your own expense."

"Then, that's the kind I want to go out under. If I'm dependent on a mission, I'll never learn to walk by faith." I continued, "God has a plan. He will lead me and meet all my needs. He has promised."

The next lesson in my faith walk was unpredicted: suddenly, my GI Bill checks stopped. When my years benefits ended, a new law said I could have a month for every month I was in the service. So, now I had a year and a half more.

I went to the VA to see why there was no check. It was just a mistake; he would trace it down. When it cleared, it would be retroactive. That was fine, but I was taking a heavy schedule and couldn't take on a job; but my bills went on. Without anyone knowing my problem besides the Lord, gifts began to come. When I gave a performance, they thought I had plenty so they didn't even pay carfare before; but now they gave me an honorarium. The term was nearly over. Then came a day when my purse was empty and I had to pay a fifty-cent fee the next day. "Lord, you answered Joy Ridderhof and Ann in such fantastic ways as they made recordings in unwritten tribal languages. My prayer partner, Margaret Schnauble, was able to tell you her needs when her missionary parents couldn't. If you can do it for them, you can do it for me. I need fifty cents tomorrow. I am making this need known only to you. I claim your promise to supply all my needs. Thank you for what you are going to do."

Biola was in the heart of downtown LA, so all doors were locked. As I dressed for classes, there in the middle of the floor was a new fifty-cent piece.

Rejoicing, I attended classes.

A couple of days later, I needed $1.00.

"Lord you gave me the fifty cents I needed, now I need one dollar." I told Him what it was for and thanked Him.

After classes, I looked in my mailbox; there was a little envelope. Inside, there was a card with a little bird, a Bible verse and a new one-dollar bill—no name, only the unseen hand of God.

School was nearly over and still my GI checks had not come through. In a few days, I was to go to northern California. "Lord, you gave me the fifty cents and the dollar, but now I can't possibly get by for less than $10.00."

None in the mail.

I finished classes and went to my room. There on the corner of my dresser was a $10.00 bill and a note from Gloria Frickey. She and Elmer were headed for India and were praying for a tropically treated accordion; mine was that kind.

"I want you to give it to her," the Lord had requested.

"Gloria, the Lord wants me to give you this. If anyone earmarks a gift toward an accordion, you may give that to help me buy another. If not, it's OK."

She wrote:

"Way up in Minnesota, a lady gave me this ten-dollar bill and said it was for my accordion. Here it is. That's all that was given. Thanks ever so much. Wish I could wait and see you, but must rush."

That ten dollars stretched like rubber to meet needs. I had to get dental work done. One of the dear men at church, a dentist, lost his wife. In his loneliness, he married a professing Christian who turned out to be a gold digger. All the joy went out of his life. As he listened to my joyful testimony, he began to smile again. The dental bill should have been at least $15.00. "Today you owe only one dollar," he grinned. "You've been a great encouragement."

Instead of storing our things in boxes in the basement for the summer, the dean demanded trunks. Mother had a friend in a big rest home. She would sell me hers for $1.00. A friend took his car to bring it back. "Oh, I don't feel like emptying it just now," she said. "Come back some other time." It was too small anyway.

The head janitor was in the hall. "Would you have any trunks to sell?" I asked.

"Follow me." Down in a very large basement was a room full of trunks. "How many do you need?"

"Nearly every girl in Biola needs a trunk."

"Pick out the ones you like best." I chose two that should cost about twenty-five dollars.

"Could you pay two dollars apiece?"

"Oh yes," I gasped. "How wonderful!"

After frequent trips leading other students to this storehouse of good trunks, they paid for mine.

The last day…the last mail came. Still no checks.

"Lord, the music store where I got my new accordion insists they don't mind waiting for payments. I've witnessed to them; they trust me. But it isn't right to go way up north and leave a debt. What if something would happen to me? Please send my checks."

He didn't. What could I do? I started down the hall. Betty Bush stepped out of her door as I passed. "Birdie, do you need a little money?" she inquired.

"Why yes, I could use some."

"My church sponsored me this year and I have $100 more than I need. It's the Lord's money; you may have it if you need it."

Tears of joy expressed my gratitude. "I only asked the Lord for $75.00 to pay off my bill. When my GI pay does come in, I can pay you back to use for next semester." Betty became a dedicated missionary in Africa.

With my bed and clothing roll and two heavy suitcases, I stopped at the dorm door. I had ten cents in my pocket. "Lord, I know I'm going, but I don't know how." There was nothing at mail time.

"Look again." He prodded. There was a ten-dollar bill and a note from the mission director's daughter:

"Sorry I forgot to give you this. Dad sent it for your bus fare."

"Praise the Lord. Now, how do I get to the bus?"

Just then, Virginia Miller—Biola's nurse last year who just married—came in with her husband, Lutch. "Where are you headed with that load?"

They called a taxi and put me on the bus with a big sack lunch. Through the night, I marvelled at God's provision.

CHAPTER 6

Applying Biblical Concepts
NEXT LESSON ON FAITH

In the morning, I tried to start a conversation with a nurse lieutenant. No response. A great field of wild flowers caused me to gasp in awe at their beauty.

"Are you interested in wild flowers?" she queried.

"Oh yes, I love all of nature."

"That's my hobby."

"One of mine, too." Soon we were sharing like old friends. The bus stopped for lunch.

"Come have dinner with me," she invited.

"I have my lunch."

"You're not going to eat your lunch, you're coming to have a good meal with me. This is Sunday. When I'm in church, I put a dollar in the offering plate. I'm putting it in a dinner plate for you this time."

By the time she was to slip on out of my sight, I had told her of the Rose of Sharon and the Lily of the Valley. With her address exchanged for mine and tears in our eyes, we parted.

The seat beside me was soon occupied by a middle-aged teacher.

"I used to go to church…I sang in the choir…but some gossips hurt my feelings and I walked out and never went back. I heard some good church music coming out of a hall where special meetings were advertised. There, the preacher was preaching to an empty hall. I felt sorry for him."

Explaining how the love of God is so much greater than the failure of sinful people, she began to hunger for more.

At Eureka, we checked in for our next bus out. There was none till six in the morning. She took me out for a fish dinner on the wharf and to spend the night with her in a hotel.

That evening, as we spent time on our knees, she poured out her need of repentance and asked the Lord to forgive her for the pride, self-pity and resentment she had let poison her heart.

I reported in the bus depot by six the next morning.

"Who told you there was a bus leaving for Hayfork this morning?"

"The man who was standing right where your shoes are standing."

"Well, that bus doesn't leave till Wednesday."

"But, I have to get there today!"

"Sorry."

"Does anything go near by?"

"The mail truck goes closest—say…thirty-five miles from it."

"I'll take it." I thought I could catch a ride that far.

An old half-ton with a cab for five people and a closed box for mail, headed east with the mailman—an old man—and three small children and Aunt Birdie. No chance to talk over the roar of the old engine, but when it stopped at every mailbox and little villages all through the day, I learned that the children had never heard the name of Jesus except as a swear word. They were going to visit their lumberjack dad.

I started from the beginning: how God made the beautiful world and put Adam and Eve in the lovely garden; but an enemy tempted them to doubt the goodness of their creator. When they believed Satan's lies, they became sinful and had to leave the delightful garden and the fellowship with God. I described the sacrifice of an innocent lamb to cover their sin—looking forward to the time God would send His Son into the world as the baby Jesus. I told of His perfect life and His trip to the cross—dying in our place—to fulfill the Law and allow us to be forgiven.

They had professed to believe and receive Jesus as their Savior before they left. With their names and address for others to follow up, I committed them to the care of the Lord.

At the end of the road, the lumber town consisted of a little shack of a store and post office, and a few rough, wooden homes.

"Is there anyone going over to Hayfork from here?" I hoped.

"There ain't a car goes over that road, ma'am, but about once a month."

"But I need to get there today."

"Wal if'n it's an emergency, I reckon the ranger would call through and see if'n somebody could come and fetch you."

Just then the ranger stepped through the door.

"It looks like this is an emergency."

He called. "How in the world did you get there?" It was the mission director who answered.

"I was directed that route in LA, but it was God's plan. I'll explain when I see you."

"I haven't been within sound of this phone in six months. I just happened in when the call came in. That's quite a road, but you wait right there till I get there."

I went out the door. A little boy was playing ball alone, so I joined him. As we played, his mother came to get him for supper.

"You say you are a missionary?" There was a sense of wonder in her voice. "And you have a vacation Bible school?"

"Yes, that is what I came to do."

"A couple of years ago, two young ladies came up here and my little girl went and she got...what she said...she got saved! After that she was so good and so happy. Could you tell me how I could get..." the magnitude of the request seemed awesome, "...how I could get saved, too?" Praise the Lord. I could.

We went to the humble little shack, and there, in the dim light of evening, the Light of the World filled her longing soul. With a testament in her hands and heavenly joy in her heart, we went out to meet the mission director.

The other students who had signed up to help with the Bible schools didn't arrive, so I went through orientation alone and for half the summer I led the Bible schools alone.although there were seventy-five to a hundred children of all ages in one room, they had never had the precious luxuries of easy-to-teach lessons and easy-to-make crafts. Parents and children were so excited over the stories from the Word and the joy of singing happy, action songs. In those days, I could do the bird songs and whistling, also. They responded to love. Many decisions for Christ were made.

The closing program after a picnic, I had the children demonstrating what they had learned and had made in crafts. An offering was taken. It was always just barely enough to get supplies and fare to my next appointment.

At the close of the largest group in Pollock Pines, as we were rejoicing in the harvest, a letter arrived from Hayfork:

> "The young people who signed up to help, finally arrived. It would save me $10.00 if I used them up here the rest of the summer. You can now go home."

"Lord, that isn't fair," I fumed. "Here I've been doing three peoples' work, and they dump me and use the unfaithful ones."

"But wasn't that what you asked for?" the Lord reminded me of my faith walk.

"Oh yes, Lord, I am trying to learn to walk by faith—not by sight. From now on, I'm not under some man's directions. I'm taking this as from you. Lead me in the way you want me to go."

CHAPTER 7

❧

Adversity Brings Courage
EXPERIENCES IN THE CALIFORNIA MOUNTAINS

Don, the missionary in that mountain area, told of a little lumber town high up that had never had a witness. Would I like to have them take me. Don and Dolores Spurbeck and their children took me into high-mountain grandeur. We met in a one-room schoolhouse. "We don't know what a vacation Bible school is, but if it's something for our kids, we want it."

"I don't have a car. Is there any place where I could stay?"

"Our homes are too small as it is. We don't have room."

"Couldn't I stay in the schoolhouse?"

"Wouldn't you be afraid?"

"No. I have the Lord looking after me." It was agreed; I'd be there two weeks.

I unrolled my bedroll, opened the windows, asked for an angel guard—if any of the men at the nearby tavern got any ideas—and prepared for the adventures the Lord had planned.

Early, every child, from birth up, and grandma, came. They were so excited, it was hard to get them to go home for meals or sleep. Soon, I was invited into the homes for meals. Parents began to catch the glimpse of joy they saw in the children.

What a thrill to see burly lumbermen and weary women marked by a rough life in the world, go down on their knees beside a davenport and ask the Savior to forgive them for their many sins and save them.

Those prayers were wondrously answered—as was evidenced in the next summer when I returned with Audrey, my missionary partner, and in years to come.

Returning to Pollock Pines, the mother of one of the little girls who had been saved there approached me, "Would you be willing to be the devotional counselor for our Girl Scout campout up in the mountains for two weeks. You get your board; your room is the open sky. You can have Sunday services and deal with any of the girls or counselors. When my girls were wanting to go into scouting, I became a leader so I could control what they were learning."

I was born in the Rockies. Love for the rugged heights is in my blood. Framed by dark, tall pines, we could almost pick the brilliant stars out of the clear sky. God kept them all in place. Lying in our bedrolls alongside my young scouts, we talked. He had the whole world in His hands; but He was so great, He had the whole universe as well.

🐦🐦🐦

The daughter of one of the counselors was to bring her horse and dog in one afternoon, but we became very concerned when she didn't show up long overdue. So her mother and I went to her starting point and followed the horse and dog tracks up the wrong trail. We came to a bald top of the highest elevation. There were no more trails, tracks or clues as to which way she went. It was getting dark and cold. We had two small flashlights and thin clothing.

"God knows where Charlotte is," I assured the panic stricken mother. "Let's just sit right down here and ask Him to lead her safely to camp and get us back, too—even if we can't locate her in the dark."

We skirted the bare rock and found a trail. Feeling our way, it lead to a fence and gate. Shadows of an old barn and house rose faintly visible. We climbed through the barbed wire. A blood-curdling scream stopped us in our tracks.

"Charlotte, Charlotte!" her mother cried. "She's in there." She started to run toward the old barn. I grabbed her.

"No, no, that isn't Charlotte," I held her back. "That's a mountain lion. If we get off that trail, we'll be lost, too. Come on."

We went back through the barbwire fence and wearily followed the two tracks. In the wee hours, we saw two headlights heading toward us. We waved the car to a stop; a cowboy was just getting back from a date. He took us to the cattle ranch. A hot cup of cocoa and warm food thawed us out. Two of the cowboys knew a shortcut to the Scout camp.

We squeezed into an open jeep and headed down—and I mean down. It almost seemed like a nose dive. We were so close to trees, at times, they should have scraped the paint off the sides. Breathlessly, Brenda ran into the camp as soon as the motor stopped.

"She's here. She just got in. The horse and dog led her down the ravine and they made it OK. She just gave the reins to the horse and he carried her on in."

How happy she was. Brenda paid the cowboys and started back across the stream to camp. "Wait a minute, Brenda," I called. "Don't you think we should stop and thank the Lord for answering our prayer?"

She returned and we knelt by a rock and expressed our gratitude for His care of all of us.

As I crawled into my sleeping bag alongside of Charlotte's younger sister, who is saved, we rejoiced in the tender loving care of her mom and sister. When her mother came near and heard us praying, tears flowed down her cheeks.

Later, I asked Brenda if she didn't want to put her trust in the Savior, too.

"I'd love to, but my husband isn't saved and that would separate us. If he would accept the Lord, then I would, too." The last time I visited them, they were still unsaved. What a tragedy. Charlotte became a lover of horses, but not a lover of God as far as I know.

Camp was over. Bears had raided our outdoor kitchen at times, and there was ice on the water in the mornings, but we all came down in healthy, happy bodies. Some had a new dimension to their lives; they could see far beyond the brilliant stars and talk to God, friend-to-friend.

CHAPTER 8

Alive By Christ

MOTHER AT MOUNT HERMON

There were still three weeks before school started. Back in Pollock Pines with the Spurbecks, mail poured in—gifts from friends; and some I didn't know or remember, remembered me. I longed for a chance to take my dear mother to a real Bible-believing conference at Mount Hermon. Here I had enough now to take her for two whole weeks of being together in a heavenly atmosphere, where she could hear the Word of God taught in all its beauty and power.

On the way down, I was waiting for Don in a little foothill town. I killed time by browsing around an old general store.

A highly painted Jewess came to wait on me. I couldn't buy anything, but I could give her something very precious. I had her ear. I explained why I was there and that the joy of knowing the Messiah was my reason for leaving the glamour world I had found repulsive.

A young man swaggered in.

"Come here," she demanded. "I want you to hear what this lady is telling me." I went on telling of the new life and victory over sin that Jesus alone can give. Another man, typical of the cocky guys in the bars, came toward her with a, "Hi, Babe."

"Be quiet and come here and listen. It will do you good."

With an audience of three, the Lord spoke to hearts who knew they were sinners and lost. Using these lips of clay, He gave them the good news that they, too, could be saved if they would only believe by putting their full weight of trust in the Lord Jesus Christ who died to pay for their sins and rose again to grant eternal life. Our Messiah died for Jews and Gentiles and He's coming again.

The two weeks at the Mount Hermon conferences was a foretaste of Heaven. Near the sea and hidden from the fast-moving world among giant Redwoods, it seemed the Lord was giving me a greater insight into the mighty God I serve. It was the first time Mother had heard real sound Bible teaching. She didn't think I was narrow-minded anymore.

Back at Biola, my GI checks were waiting for me. There was enough to pay Betty the $75.00 I owed her, my tuition and expenses, and enough more to buy an organ for a missionary friend working with lepers in Africa. Now they could learn to play and sing to the Lord. If my prayer had been answered the way I begged the Lord—to send my check on time so I could pay my way through the summer—I would have missed the thrill of having needs met by the loving hand of my Abba, Father.

CHAPTER 9

Applying Biblical Concepts
BACK TO BIOLA

While at Biola, I sought out students who might be lonely or have some special needs.

One girl was poorly dressed and often walked alone. After prayer for her, I gave her my best pen-and-pencil set and the only good pair of hose I owned. Instead of accepting my offer of friendship, she avoided me. Later, she came to ask my forgiveness. The Lord was dealing with her because of her jealousy of me.

"Many times I was tempted to throw the pen and pencil on the floor and stamp on them because you had so much that you could give away—expensive things like that. And you greeted so many with 'Honey.' No one calls me 'Honey.' I almost hated you."

"I'm sorry you misunderstood me. When the Lord asked me to give you a love gift, He told me to give you my best set and best stockings. My others I had mended so much they weren't fit to give. I wanted to be your friend." The rest of the semester, we sat together when we could.

A beautiful friendship was established with Dr. Lee and Tien Chu Chang of Taiwan. They had escaped the Communist takeover and felt the need of more Bible knowledge. With their extra barrier of limited English, most students avoided them— not knowing how to communicate. Tien Chu knew that her brother had gone with the Communists. He tried to get her to return to China to visit her "sick" mother; but she knew it was a trick to get her to return to be killed, so she adopted my old mother as a substitute. Later, Audrey and I took Mother and her on a trip from Seattle to Yellowstone and on, until we put her and Doris Newman on a bus back to Biola and we went on to Lincoln with mother.

While at Biola, they took me to a Chinese restaurant. The table was loaded with foods strange to me, but very good. When I could eat no more, Dr. Lee said, "Eat. It's all paid for." I demonstrated with my hand I was full to the top of my neck. They called for containers and filled them, saying it is a compliment to the cook when all the food is eaten or taken. I ate a week on the leftovers. They were dear friends.

One year, my practical works assignment took me to the huge juvenile hall of Los Angeles. It was the size of a big city block with big, three-story buildings spaced around an exercise yard. Each Lord's Day, I spent nearly all day going from department to department. They were from babies to sixteen. The little ones were usually there while parents were in prison; the older ones were guilty of major crimes.

They were asked why they committed the offenses. Often they would say they saw it done in the movies or read about how to do it in the "comics," and tried it out themselves. A large percent were of the Roman Catholic religion, going to mass and to confession, but continued in sin. Very few of the rest of them had ever been in a Sunday school.

One of the girls who came to trust in the Savior was a teen by the name of Dianne. She had been caught forging checks and was a Federal case because she was from Canada. She was a joy to work with—reading Bible portions and memorizing

Scripture. She had read through the New Testament and learned the required verses to get a King James Bible.

"I want a Protestant Bible," she insisted.

"She can't have one; she's a Catholic," the matron was insistent. Dianne was angry.

"Dianne, have you read all the material I gave you?"

"No."

"You have enough of the Bible to study until you get out of here, so you just wait. I'll see that you get your Bible then," I assured her. "I don't feel sorry for you. You have Jesus in your heart now and your matron doesn't. She's still as lost like you were. Pray for her and live for Jesus so she'll want the new joy you have."

The next week the matron met me, "I don't know what you told Dianne. She used to be the worst girl I had, but now she's the best. I've decided she should have the Bible she wants.

Another of the teens was placed in solitary confinement. She asked for me to visit her. I was locked in a triangular vestibule. They told me to look through the bars into the cell on the right before I went in to Mary's. There lay a girl, unconscious. The space was cluttered with plaster. In super-human strength, she had torn her bed to shreds, torn plaster off half the wall and crumpled the metal lath. It took powerful men to overcome her and shoot drugs into her till she passed out. I was reminded of the demoniac who broke chairs and bonds till Jesus healed him. She had to have been strengthened by demonic power.

The remote control opened the door to Mary's cell. We sat on the iron bunk and, with arm around her, told of the love of Jesus that was waiting for her if she put her trust in Him alone. She shouldn't go to the Virgin Mary to persuade her Son to hear her prayers. She had His loving attention all the time. She could confess to Jesus that she was a sinner and ask Him to forgive her. When she accepted His death on the cross to pay for all her sins, He became her Savior and she became His child. He would never leave her or forsake her. She wouldn't be alone in the cell anymore. With new hope, she became a new child of God.

Sometime later, I was asked to give a message in a halfway house for boys. Several ran to greet me as I drove up. "Do you remember us? You used to teach us at juvenile hall. We all accepted the Lord, and we are pals and help each other live like Christians." Often, I've been rewarded by meeting children who were touched by the Holy Spirit as I gave them the gospel. From delinquents, they were transformed into zealous representatives of God's grace—what a thrill!

Miss Clark, a retired missionary, was taking care of my mother part of the time while I was at Biola. She lived in Arcadia, an LA suburb. I visited her as often as possible; she never wanted to let me go. One night, the last streetcar was due, she clung to me until I had to run to catch it.

I was almost at the stop when it came. I yelled, whistled and ran after it, but it disappeared. I ran a couple of blocks to another line. Fortunately, two women were waiting. Out of breath, I climbed in and sat beside an older lady and behind the two. "Where are you going so late?" one asked.

"I'm a student at Biola. I've just been to visit my mother."

"Biola! I suppose you listen to Dr. Talbut on the radio. Well, let me tell you something: He's a heretic. He doesn't believe that America is one of the toes on the beast in Daniel."

"It isn't important to know who the toes represent," I responded. "It is important to be sure you are born again because the Bible says, 'All have sinned,' and, 'The wages of sin is death, but the gift of God is eternal life through Jesus Christ our Lord.'"

The irate woman raved on and on about her pastor being the only one who was right. I just quietly repeated scriptures. As I got off in the center of the city, she called after me, "You go on to hell with that movie crowd." Two theaters were just emptying.

As I stepped to the curb, I noticed one of the ladies following me. I stopped. "Is it a sin to commit suicide?"

"Oh yes, you would become a murderer. God's Law says, 'Thou shalt not murder.' Whether you kill yourself or another, you are destroying a life that only God has a right to end."

There on the crowded corner, she shared her sad story. Her son had been disabled in the war, but, for some reason, refused compensation; her husband had died; and her priest insisted he should lay with her.

"I loved my husband," she wept. "I can't feel he has the right, even if he is a priest."

When the gospel was explained to her, she opened her heart to the Savior who would meet her needs; she was directed to the source of growth and fellowship with true Christians.

My late return to Biola was excused. I had another lesson in God's great plan (Romans 8:28).

The talent God gave me for bird imitations and whistling solos opened many exciting new doors. There were around three thousand children at a child evangelism rally; there was Youth for Christ and other large ministries. I was at the head table at a conference in my first year at Biola.

"Who is that distinguished-looking gentleman in the center?" I asked my accompanist.

"Oh, don't you know?" That's Charles Fuller of the Old Fashioned Revival Hour. He's the speaker this evening.

Remembering my hunger for spiritual food after I met Jesus as my Lord, I heard him on radio. One of my great desires was to go to Long Beach some Saturday and join the four thousand who were drawn to the Lord through that outstanding servant. Here I was, almost arm's length from him. When he got up to speak, many asked him to sing the theme song, "Heavenly Sunshine."

"I will if the Bird Girl will whistle it with me."

Being head and shoulders taller, they put a box for me to stand on so we could use the mike together. Much later, he was speaking to the thousand students; as he awaited his time, he looked at me and waved. I couldn't believe it was for me, but, as soon as it was over, he strode down the aisle and reached out his big hand, "How's the Bird Girl?"

Another joy was being in Dr. McGee's church and home before he became my teacher at Biola, my pastor at the Church of the Open Door, and, later, a personal friend. Getting to know a number of God's greats challenged me to press on for the high calling of His plan for me.

After two years of seminary, friends from Africa Inland Mission wanted me to change into Christian Education so I could graduate before I was 40. I already had a degree and teachers' college and years of experience. They said I didn't need another degree.

I'd had a hard time with Greek, although I loved the wonderful new depths of understanding our professor taught. But, I felt I couldn't master Hebrew, so it was easy to talk me out of a theological degree.

That year, I studied the needs of missionary kids and their schooling, with Africa as a goal. Beside my full schedule, I spent time with Mother and did lots of speaking, whistling and bird songs in conferences and churches. When I was given the physical required by AIM, I didn't pass. I had some indigestion from overworking.

"We need you at Riethie." Friends wanted me to try again with a different doctor. "He's just too particular."

"No, I never force a door open. If God wants me in Africa, He will open the door."

"Aren't you upset or disappointed?"

"No, not in the least," I assured them. "God is in charge. He opens the right door in His time. I just wait and listen and obey."

Audrey Friedel was in the senior class with me. She had me speak to the large group of young people in her church. Streetcar connections from there were poor, so I had to get back to the dorm late. The next time, she arranged for me to stay with her in her parents' home. We had to sleep on the davenport after the rest were in bed. She couldn't use her younger sister's beautiful room while she was away in college. She opened a can of spaghetti for her meal and her mother scolded her harshly, "I bought that for your sister."

"But I didn't have anything to eat, and I was hungry. I'll replace it."

I saw she was a nervous wreck trying to please her rich-but-godless family. They were using and abusing her, but she took it in her attempt to win them to Christ.

"She'll not last out this year," I told the dean of women. "She works from daylight to dark for her folks all the time she isn't in class. Can't we give her a room here in school so she can graduate?"

"There isn't a bed in any of the double rooms."

"I hate to give up the privacy of my little single room, but I can't see her destroyed. You can put a double deck in mine. It'll be a tight fit, but it's only for a semester."

The story of her conversion and rejection, all she had been through because of her stand for Christ, would warrant another biography. I admired her faithfulness.

During the summer I was serving alone, I had VBS in Auberry, CA. The Lord blessed with conversions and lifelong friends—Lorna Wiley was one. She had been raised in liberal churches and accepted the Savior in VBS, but had no nurturing in the Word of God. She brought her two children and heard the plain gospel that Christ died for her sins and must be the living Lord in her heart. The children loved me so much that they claimed me as their "other mother."

Lorna became my most faithful friend and prayer warrior. She came to visit me at Biola for a few days. As she left, her little Ann kissed her and said she would pray that Jesus would take care of her; but if anything happened and

Jesus took her to heaven; she would be Aunt Birdie's little girl. Her prayers were the sweetest visit with Jesus I've ever heard.

My final exam in systematic theology was harder than this old brain was capable of passing. We had a brilliant professor and I was thrilled with all I was learning, but try as I would, hour after hour, quoting the proof texts perfectly with references for all the doctrines in the Bible was beyond my ability. It was a five-hour class. If I didn't pass I wouldn't graduate.

"Lord, I've done the very best I can to prepare for that exam tomorrow. You promised in Philippians 4:19 to supply all my needs. That is a need!"

At ten o'clock next day, I sat at the desk with pages before me and an unmarked Bible. I went leafing through the pages. My mind went blank. Through my frightened days as a child, at test times my mind would blank out—a mental block would keep me from reciting or answering questions I knew as well as my name. Why was this happening to me now?

I opened my Bible, "Lord, I still claim your promise. In Ephesians 3:20 and 21a, I saw that He is able to do exceeding abundantly above all I ask or think, according to the power that works in me, unto you be the glory."

It seemed God's calm was flowing into me, and He was guiding my hand. For the next two hours, I was answering the questions. At noon, I handed the paper in. No wonder I got one of the highest grades in the class—God wrote my exam for me. To Him be all the glory!

A letter arrived from Lorna:

> What was happening to you between ten o'clock and noon on Friday? The Lord stopped me in my ironing and told me to get on my knees and pray for you. I was praying for two hours and then I was sure everything was all right.

In the years to come, she was so in tune with the Lord that every time I was in danger or in need she was called to pray at the exact time of my need.

❦ ❦ ❦

"Will you take this money to the office for me," Audrey asked as she rushed off to work. "See how much more I owe."

I had to go myself, so I asked the casheer how much I owed. She checked.

"Oh, you are all paid up. Someone has given the rest."

"Then see how much Audrey owes. Maybe I can pay hers." She checked.

"It's paid in full, too."

Praise the Lord! Now there was hope of owning a car for the work He had called us to do.

Right after the door closed to Africa, Mrs. Helen Duff Baugh spoke in behalf of the Christian Business and Professional Women's Club and the teams of girls they sponsored to go out to the little towns where there was no church, or a dead one. I had spent the last summer doing that type of ministry and saw how very rewarding it was.

"This is where I want you," the Lord spoke to my heart.

As Audrey met me on her way to work, she asked if I'd set up an appointment for her to speak to Mrs. Baugh, for God was calling her to go. She was thrilled to hear that I had heard the same call. I hadn't known that she had spent a summer with the same mission years before.

I went to the designated office. Mrs. Baugh was sitting behind a desk. Half a dozen girls sat in a half-circle around her. She pointed a long finger at me, "You're Juanita McComb, aren't you?"

"Yes."

"We've just been praying you'd walk through that door."

Part of my biography had been written up for Power Magazine and Counselor. A number of letters came from readers. One from the CB&P Women's Club came from the secretary telling about the need for teachers in the villages.

"Reading about you, I was impressed you would fit that need perfectly. We're not allowed to ask anyone to join, but I hope you'll pray about it." At that time, I was thinking Africa; but God was planning neglected areas of America.

That evening, Mrs. Baugh met with both of us, "Would you like to go out as a team?"

"We have no preference; we only want God's will. Whatever you decide we will consider the leading of the Lord," we promised. So we were to go out together.

CHAPTER 10

Affliction Brings Comfort
WE START OUT WITH ENOCH

We had to have a car, and cars were hard to come by after the war that is—one within our price range. One of the students got us a dilapidated '29 Chevy. We named it "Enoch" because we hoped it wouldn't die.

I took my friend Ruth Smith along to get my driver's license. The examiner got in. We turned a corner and got half a block, and it quit in the middle of the road. "Well," the guy fumed, "you've gotta have a car that will run before you take your test." He got out and walked off.

"Now what do I do, Lord?"

A farmer kindly pushed me off the center of the road. I went after Ruth—a better mechanic than most men. She opened the hood.

"It's the fuel pump," she decided. "I think I can get it back to Biola, and we'll get a pump and install it. By choking it, we went in spurts back to school.

Soon, the new pump was installed; I got my license. For three days and most of the night, we carefully sorted out the things we would need for winter and summer, for meetings, for children, women and families. No room for anything not important.

By Sunday evening, all was packed and I went after the car. As I stood just outside the dorm door, I had reached such exhaustion I couldn't take another step.

"Lord," I prayed, "I've got to start VBS in Auberry by 9 o'clock in the morning. You promised, 'As thy day so shall thy strength be.'" As if an electric shock coursed through my body, power went from feet to head. I was renewed! When I double-parked the little old '29 Chevy, Audrey rolled a dolly alongside. Several thousand people were passing us and entering the Church of the Open Door. Some stopped and shook heads.

"Do you plan to put that in that?" The pile of luggage looked bigger than the car.

"I hope so," I told them. "We need it all. If I can't pack it in, I'll have to ship it."

By the time church was over, I had all of it in or on that car. A mummy case was just right to hold bedroll, clothing and shoes. One end was tied on. "Now all I need is enough rope to tie the front end on."

A man ran to his car and produced the right length rope. As friends shook hands and wished us God's blessings, many left small gifts of money. One lady gave a check. God knew exactly how much we would need until the offering after vacation Bible school.

That night, there wasn't a time I wasn't facing car lights. They were building a new highway over the mountains, so bad detours made the going very hard and slow. My eyes gave out, so I rested them while Audrey did up my hair.

By dawn, we reached Fresno and headed toward the hills. We pulled up at the church just at nine o'clock. Lorna and friends were there ready to help. Audrey couldn't drive, so she got some sleep on the way. So, I let her take over that afternoon, organizing the helpers while I slept.

The Wileys had a big basement, so we were able to store things for the seasonal changes. Wayne helped unload, "Don't touch anything until I take a picture of that pile of stuff they had in that car. The fellows at work won't believe it, unless I prove it."

Next morning he greeted us, "I put your spare on. You had a flat, and I knew you'd be in a hurry to go. You better drop this one off at the garage on your way."

When we returned, "I put a new tube in that tire," the mechanic explained, "I knew you'd want one. Have a look at this." He picked up the old tube and tore it like a piece of paper.

"If that tube is like that, we better have a look at the rest." We had been riding on three tires with tubes as rotten as old paper. The Lord had brought us over those bad roads all night and kept us rolling with that heavy load. Praise the Lord!

All through that first year, we experienced many dangers but we had confidence that the Lord was our protector and that He had appointed Lorna to hold us up in prayer.

We went to Cannon Beach for conferences and stayed on till we could get our programs all planned. Our first full schedule was at Dick Patti's home in Amity, Oregon. The three churches were without pastors, so he got the congregations to unite for special meetings. We had the women's Bible study at one church, the children at another and the family at the other in the evenings.

The Spirit of God was doing His work in hearts. Souls came to know the Lord, some were called to full-time ministries—some became great missionaries. Doris Newman became Mrs. Bob Baker after graduating from Biola. Her brother, Jean, and all but young Paul gave their lives in West Irian opening the hearts of a tribe to the gospel.

Before we would finish a fortnight of meetings, we'd have a call from another village. The next three years, we were kept busy in California, Oregon, Washington, Idaho and Montana. We were in lumber and fishing areas usually. In some places, we were lavished with love and appreciation, and people competed with each other to serve the best meals; the next place, often, hospitality was unknown. A can of soup could be shared to compensate for eating too much the weeks before.

We received only $50.00 a month from the clubs for all expenses. The weeks the car broke down would be the times we were fed by others. When we had to buy food, Enoch would hold up. Many times, we went for miles when the gauge said empty, and the car would stop at a gas pump on a ranch or in town. "You're doing a good work," they would say. "While you are here we want to supply the gas."

🐦🐦🐦

Audrey's well-to-do parents had mistreated her even as a child, because she was cross-eyed, until they finally had them corrected. They used her to care for the old grandma, especially as she was losing her sight. Audrey read the Bible to her.

"I like to have you read to me, but I don't like your explanations." She was a proud little woman who kept up with the latest novels.

Shortly before we left, one day Audrey was listening to Dr. Fuller on the Old Fashioned Revival Hour. Grandma stormed into the kitchen, "That man said I should get down on my knees and ask Jesus to come into my heart. Do you think I will do that? No! No! No!" She stamped her little foot.

"Audrey," her dad commanded, "you're upsetting your grandmother. Shut it off!"

After graduation, we were rescuing some of Audrey's flannelgraphs her dad had put under his lapidary wheels; water and silt had ruined most. She cried.

"Don't worry, I have plenty," I assured. That night God gave me the chance to give Grandma the gospel. As she was ready to sleep, I asked if she would like me to pray for her. Kneeling by her bed, I held her hands and asked the Lord to open her heart and prepare her for heaven.

Next morning, the Catholic nurse laughed. "Grandma said she pretended to be asleep, but she wasn't. That was just what she needed."

We were in Northern California when word came, "Grandma has fallen. She isn't going to live much longer. We will just have her cremated. You know how we hate anything pertaining to death. Don't come. We want you to remember her as she used to be. Her mind is gone. Now all she wants to listen to is Dr. Fuller and the Rescue Mission."

"Audrey, this is the time for you to go to your grandma before she dies," I insisted. We started the long trip to LA. But halfway, little old Enoch quit. I put her on a bus and stayed while men worked long after dark to get the car repaired. I told them stories of our experiences.

The job done, they crawled out of the pit. One man faced me. "No one ever loved me that much," he sighed. Our stops were as important as our go's. Enoch always stopped where someone was ready to hear the good news. I think of that man as I read in the Scriptures, "No man careth for my soul." But God does, and so do I.

Audrey reached home. Her parents said Grandma had been in a coma most of the time. Audrey went in. "Grandma, I've come."

She opened her eyes, "Oh, Audrey, are you winning any souls for Jesus?" They were in tears. Most of the week, Grandma was able to fellowship with her, then she went back into the vestibule to heaven. By the time Audrey got back, word came that she had met her Savior at ninety-four years of age.

One night after an evening meeting, the Lord burdened me for the mother of one of the little girls who had been saved. They were to move away. That was our last chance to give her the gospel. We drove thirty-five miles, got her out of bed and shared our burden for her soul.

In sub-zero weather on icy roads, our tank was on empty on our return. We stopped at a friend's place. They had only kerosene. That took us back safely.

We heard of a power-house community. A road-maintenance friend took us in his jeep over the ice-covered roads, where one slip would be the last one. The mothers knew their kids were lacking moral standards and talked of starting a Sunday school, but no one knew how.

Sitting in the living room of a leading family, I saw a canary. I started imitating their song; the bird chimed in. It was so excited, they opened the cage and he flew directly to me. On my shoulder, when I turned toward it, he put his beak to my lips—like a kiss. He had never fallen in love before, and they had a hard time getting him back in his cage.

The children were excited about our meetings. One of the teachers had a spare bedroom. Trusting the omnipotent hand of our Father, we crossed the icy mountain roads.

As we were setting up for the first evening, Bee, the teacher, sat at the piano and played a classical Russian number like a professional pianist.

"Wonderful! Will you play for our meetings?"

"No," emphatically. "I couldn't even play 'Holy, Holy, Holy.'" We had prepared for the musical accompaniment on a wire recorder, so we had that to meet our needs.

After the meeting, Bee took us to the teacherage. She sat on our bed and laughed at jokes and fun stories we shared.

The meetings went well; the children were like sponges and soaked it all in.

The second evening as we were together in our bedroom, the Lord led into the serious condition of Bee's soul. We showed her God's provision for her salvation.

As she went to her room, we heard sobs. I went in and put my arm around her, "What is it, Bee? May I help you?"

"Down in LA, I had no power to resist sin in my life. I took this job thinking I could get away from temptation, but it has followed me. So I've been wanting to end it all. I planned to take my life…then, you came."

"Bee, it won't help to take your own life by your own hand. What you need is eternal life at God's hand. He wants to save you and give you a clean, new heart. That's why Jesus came to earth, to save sinners just like you. He died on the cross to pay for your sins. If you let Him come into your heart, He will give you a new way of life and the power to resist sin."

The next afternoon, Bee's students went home saying, "We have a new teacher." They saw the radiant new life that had blossomed. Many of the children put their trust in the Savior that week. When they saw parents gambling, they tried to tell them it was sin.

We hadn't said one word about drinking, smoking or gambling. It was the believing children who recognized it as wrong.

Guilty parents said, "A little religion is OK, but when they start meddling in our business, that's going too far. The girls have to get out of the schoolhouse for their meetings."

"They can meet in my house, then," Bee wanted more, so the meetings continued the following week. Those who came to trust the Lord, grew warm; the others grew cold.

"Come on up to the higher dam. We need you, too," came the call.

"We can give you only one week." We went. God blessed. After we had to go, a heaven-sent revival took over; reports were thrilling.

As I reminisce, my memory bank recalls several other villages where the Lord did a unique work. One was the lumber mill at Camby, California. Going north from Redding, we thought we'd never get there. After hoping the light ahead would mean journey's end, we were disappointed. Hopefully, Audrey pointed to a sparkled horizon. "Is that it?" Audrey sighed.

"Can be!"

It was.

Camby was located on high, table land where winter came early and strong winds whipped across the prairie. Mill men were mostly Okies and Arkies who had lost everything in the Midwest dust-bowl era and escaped to the West seeking any kind of work. There were ranchers and the few white-collar folks, but most were poor—and they loved to share.

"If they can eat it, I can too." I tried to encourage Audrey to try new combinations. If we were picky, we would hurt the feelings of our hostesses who offered us their very best. One meal, stewed chicken was dished into soup bowls. Audrey saw a head with two little eyes looking up at her. When no one was looking, she slipped it into my dish.

We identified well with the poor as we drove old Enoch. There was such an increase of interest through the two weeks, that the people enlarged the little church, called a young pastor and placed an old boxcar as a home for us to use the next spring. The young pastor was not well-liked, so the work on the church lagged behind. He didn't announce the VBS or prepare for our meetings. But when we pulled into town, the kids all shouted for joy. We needed no other advertising. The whole town turned out. We named our boxcar quarters The Manshun.

One dear Christian couple lived on a ranch several miles away. They became our loved ones for whom we'd go miles out of our way to stay with—open door, open hearts.

Mabel, while out of fellowship with the Lord, had married this rough cowboy. When she paid dearly for her willful rejection of God's warning about being unequally yoked, she tried to lead him to the Savior. He seemed almost demon-possessed, until he was thrown from a horse and got a glimpse of the awful fires of hell. After his conversion, he was as on fire for the Lord as he had been for the devil.

A widow, Esther, with a young son, was about to marry Frank, a navy friend of her husband who had been killed in an accident. Frank had wheat growing on the land he had cleared. He felled timber and worked in the mill. He was faithful in church and loved to sing. Esther was assured he was a Christian, but the men at the mill saw him through the week.

Mabel and her husband invited us out to the ranch, hoping we could lead him to the true faith. "He's headstrong; a hard nut to crack. Hope you can get through to him without making him angry," they warned.

Mabel was one wonderful cook. After the pleasant visit Frank started to leave. I followed him out to the gate. "Frank, do you know the difference between a professing Christian and a possessing Christian?"

He didn't understand what I meant. He had been sprinkled as a baby, joined a church, sang in the choir and even put money in the offering. Wasn't that enough?

I explained the gospel in John 3. Jesus told a very religious man he wouldn't see or enter the kingdom of Heaven without being born again. He was born physically into a sinful body that would soon perish. Unless he put his whole weight of trust in the Lord Jesus Christ who died on the cross to pay for his sins, he would have to pay for them in hell. If he accepted the gift of God described in John 3:16, his sins would be forgiven and he would be born again spiritually.

He promised to prayerfully read the New Testament, making very sure he was a possessing Christian. He kept his promise.

The sequel to that story will appear later.

After our weeks at Camby, we went farther north to Likely. We stayed on a cattle ranch with a precious middle-aged couple who had recently met Christ via radio. When they sent for literature, one of the leaders of that sect made many trips to teach them, get them to join their group and start tithing. They began to search the Scriptures and discovered many errors in his teaching. When they refused to join, he tried to get her to secretly join—then she could try to get her husband to follow. Angered at his godless attempts to force them, they forced him to leave them alone.

That opened the door for us to come in with the pure Word of God. We opened up the little closed church that had served as a community hall. The young pastor, who was trying to serve two villages, lit the oil stove and left. As we came from the children's story hour, the church was full of smoke. I ran in with our small fire extinguisher, while Audrey ran to the store for their large one. Oil had filled a drip pan under the heater. It was controlled before the building was harmed.

As we followed the young pastor, right after we got the fire out, we saw him stop and throw dirt on his engine. His car was on fire. Fortunately, we had replaced the fire extinguisher we had just used up. It was evident we faced satanic forces, so we asked praying friends to join us in this spiritual warfare. At the end of our two weeks, many marveled at the transformations in lives that were enslaved by alcohol, cults, or depression. His almighty power and love won their hearts. The dear ranchers where we stayed became strong students of the Word and leaders in the little church.

Another community said no one would come to our VBS. The children were scattered for vacation. But we convinced the leaders of the dead little church to let us start anyway; children came out of the woodwork. Grandparents collected their grandchildren. Before the two weeks ended, we were sharing the good news with around three hundred. New life and enthusiasm entered the hearts of the discouraged pastor and his wife.

At another village, we were entertained by a teacher who was single. She caught the spirit of joy as we did fun things each evening, always leading to the theme that explained the way to a good life for those who believed.

They all invited us to their Halloween party at the community hall. We envisioned the normal entertainment: drinking, dancing and smoking. "If you come, we will make it a nice party," they urged. We didn't promise.

The three of us donned brightly-dyed, long-handled underwear, stuffed here and there in grotesque shapes. I made masks out of brown paper sacks, and a sign: "The Three Musty Tears." We went to the party huddled under an old umbrella. No one ever dreamed who was clowning in those funny costumes.

Audrey would try to hang up the umbrella on a peg that wasn't there. I sat on a plank that was balanced on a barrel like a teeter-totter. Children jumped on the high end, and I rolled on the floor and tried again. Everyone was laughing hilariously. Then we went backstage, put a blanket over a card table and dressed like a dwarf cowboy. With a cowboy hat, shirt, bandanna and false teeth made from an orange peel, my hands became the legs and feet while Audrey's arms were in the shirt. Thus, I told a ridiculously funny story.

They still didn't recognize their missionaries until we came out in our right minds and made orange-peel false teeth for all the ladies to wear as they served the refreshments. Those folks never forgot that Halloween and have far more enjoyment in life than those who are limited to the world's boring entertainment.

It was late fall when we went to Davis, California. That was before the AG College was built. The little old church had no pastor and few attended. We had no money for VBS craft supplies.

"What can we do?" Audrey asked.

"I'll show you. Come on."

We drove to the town dump. "You're going to get stuff here? You don't get me out of the car," she scolded.

"You'll see," I started picking up large cans I could cut open for tin-tapping projects. I came back with an electric roaster, minus the lid.

"This will be great to hold water for washing."

"Did you find that there?" She got out and came back excited. She found boxes of nails, screws, hammer heads—all sorts of good stuff from some man's shop that had just been left there in boxes waiting for us.

The Lord provided all we needed for crafts.

I gave the electric roaster to Audrey for a wedding present and, later, took some of the shop junk to Ireland with me and made good use of it.

We were given a big sugar-sack full of out-dated bakery stuff a farm friend had picked up for stock food. The next day there was a bakery strike and we were the only ones with plenty of bread.

One night after I had done a chalk painting to illustrate my message, the church was dark except for the spotlight on my picture. I invited anyone to pray who wished. A man's voice, new to us, talked to God as an intimate friend. We could hardly wait till the lights were on. Who was this newcomer?

A burly, bearded man greeted us. "I couldn't stay away any longer," he apologized.

"I got a rash on my face and had to let my beard grow. I looked so awful, I stayed home; but when I heard what you were doing, I had to come." After that we became good friends—visiting in their ranch home, hearing the thrilling story of their conversions.

She had been a dancer in a night club and he had been a boxer. He told how he tried to gain merit with God by entertaining the priests with boxing matches. He said priests were the hardest to work with because they had to breathe the smoke-filled air.

He had an exquisite singing voice. He listened to a quartet of gospel singers, then listened to their message, made contact, and became a new man. Later, he joined the quartet.

But his wife thought he was crazy. She gave him a bad time. He just kept loving her and praying, until she surrendered her religious heritage that had no power to set her free from sin and came all out for the all-powerful God who could forgive all her sins and give her the power not to sin.

Her father-in-law had bought a ranch, but he knew nothing about running it. About to lose it, Chuck and his wife came up to try to save his investment. Then, she and her mother went to LA to sell their home. While waiting for a buyer, she attended a child evangelism training school. Her mother accompanied her, reluctantly. The very last day, the Holy Spirit quickened her mother's heart. That day, the house sold and they returned rejoicing. The Christian Science husband was furious and refused to live with them; so he took off.

Years later, I was speaking in a church in New York. "Do you remember a couple of new Christians in Davis?"

"Chuck!" I exclaimed. We hugged. Now he was head of a Christian organization for boys. They were full-time for the Lord.

We were several weeks in the John Day country in eastern Oregon. Fox stands out in memory—it was just a wide place along the prairie road. An old church on a knoll spoke of better days. Now, decay depicted the condition of the community.

We waded through the tall grass. Pushing open the sagging door, I made my way behind the pulpit. "Lord," I prayed, "we claim this church for you." I looked around at broken windows, a leaky roof and years of debris. It would be impossible to get this fixed up for our meetings.

"God," I said, "Open the door of your choice and the hearts of the people; and again feed these poor people on the pure Word of God."

We were given the dance hall. We cleaned out the mess the dance crowd left on Saturday and, for two weeks, it became a sanctuary where burdened souls found the Burden Bearer.

Fay was an alcoholic trying to mother a large family. She tried desperately to overcome her addiction. Nothing helped until she put her whole body, soul and spirit into the arms of the Great Physician. I still have a card and pretty hankie that she gave me as an expression of gratitude for introducing her and her family to the new life they now enjoy.

Another transformation that demonstrated the mighty power of God, was a helpless alcoholic, Thelma—the daughter of the owner of a store and dance hall. He had institutionalized her, spent lots on cures and shock treatments, to no avail. When she walked into the hall the first time, she looked like a wild woman—glassy eyes, unkempt hair, demented! My flesh was repulsed, but my spirit said, Go and hug her.

"I died for Thelma," the Lord reminded me. "Love her to me."

We did. At first, we wondered if anything penetrated as she continued to sit in the front row. Over and over we played Stuart Hamblin's popular song:

The Chimes of Time Ring Out the News
Another day is through
Someone slipped and fell,
Was that someone you?
If you have longed for added strength
Your courage to renew
Do not be disheartened
For I have news for you.
It is no secret what God can do.
What He's done for others
He'll do for you
With arms wide open
He'll pardon you
It is no secret, what God can do.

Fay and Thelma listened to that recording over and over again till they had it memorized and believed.

We went on to other meeting places, but continued to rejoice in the powerful impact of the gospel in Fox. Fay and Thelma were especially held before the Lord in prayer.

As we went through Fox later we saw the churchyard had been mowed. We went up to the door and listened, "We gotta get this church cleaned up and ready to start a Sunday school for our kids." To the rhythm of swishing brooms, those two new creatures in Christ sang their favorite song, "It is No Secret What God Can Do."

CHAPTER 11

A Blessed Conversion

ON THE ROAD WITH MOTHER, AUDREY AND ENOCH

My mother became dependent upon me. Different friends kept her while I was on the mission field, but there were times we took her from one place to another. The year we drove Enoch, we took her along to Cannon Beach for our conference; Highway 101 was very narrow and poor in those days.

A big lumber truck would pass us and we'd pass him so often we would beep. I was ahead as we wound down a steep road skirting the sea. A car behind honked. If he tries to pass here he'll endanger us both, I thought and went a little faster.

At the bottom, I pulled off and motioned him past. He stopped and pointed. For all three miles, the back wheel on the sea's side was rolling along far out on the axle shaft. We had an extra heavy load. Again, the Lord protected.

The big truck screeched to a stop. "It's against the rules to take a rider, but I can't leave a lady in distress." I climbed way up to the cab. "What brings you to Oregon?"

"I'm a missionary. We go into little towns where they don't have any church or Sunday school."

"Maybe you can help me." He was alert. "How can I raise my little girl in such a way that she won't turn out to be like her mother?"

He explained that, as a trucker, he had to be gone from home a lot. His wife had run off with another man. "Now all I have to live for is my little daughter."

"If you bring her to Sunday school, she isn't apt to someday be brought up in court. It isn't enough to send her; you must go with her. You can't take your child any higher than you are, but neither of you can go to heaven unless you are born again." I explained the simple plan of salvation.

Letting me out by a tow truck, we thanked each other. His eyes filled with tears.

On the way back, the tow-truck driver fumed, "Preachers, missionaries—they're a bunch of hypocrites. They're gold diggers, they are. Got no use for the lot of ' em."

"Lord," I prayed, "I'm not going to ask any favors of him if I have to sell all I've got." It would have been a simple matter to turn the car right there and head for town, but he hauled it all that three miles up and back. "Oh Lord, he's running up the bill on purpose," I cried inside.

I shared some stories of changed lives of some who had embraced the gospel.

He left the car in a rickety old garage across the street and went to write out the bill. Pen in hand, he hesitated and looked up at me, "Do you suppose $10.00 would be OK?" I nearly fainted.

"Oh, thank you. Thank you. And thank you, Lord."

The mechanic leaned against the car, puffing a cigarette. "I've got three cars in ahead of yours and I don't feel very good. I won't look at yours till I get these done." It didn't look promising.

I sent Audrey and Mother to see if they could get a cheap room. It was off-season so they got a motel room for $1.00. While they rested, I stood in the waiting room. His wife, dressed in soiled jeans, was behind the counter. We began visiting. She picked up a letter opener with a little red-devil handle. "That's a picture of my husband," she sneered.

I laughed, "If you think that's a picture of the devil, your sadly mistaken. He poses as an angel of light, enticing, but he's a liar. Would you like to have me show you what God has told us?" She would. I went and got my Panorama Bible Course and began in Genesis, and followed the bloodline of Christ. The rest of the day, she stood absorbed. The children came and went—eating a slice of bread or apple, listening, or playing.

Next morning, we continued until she understood and opened her heart to the God who became a man to save her. I gave her a Testament, some literature and ways to find fellowship. It had been twenty-four hours from the time we came in. God was in charge.

We got three miles down the road when the wheel came off again. "Praise the Lord. It came off close enough to make him do it over," I hitched a ride back.

My new sister-in-Christ came along. "I'll weld it this time and it won't come off," he promised, returning for the wheel.

While I was gone, a big red truck had pulled up as Audrey and Mother flagged traffic on a curve. Audrey began to tell him some of our adventures in serving the Lord. He was deeply moved. While we waited there, this brand new Christian gave her first testimony. She was a new person.

The trucker said, "God stopped me here. My cousin wanted me to join him at Biola this fall, but I chose making money. I've been miserable. Now I know I must yield to my Lord."

After they all left, we circled arms around Mother for a praise service before going on.

As we hurried on that night, it was so foggy Audrey leaned out one door and I leaned out the other in order to keep on the road. Even within Cannon Beach, familiar territory, we couldn't find the gate. We pulled off and let Mother have the front seat, while we squeezed between the luggage and roof of the car.

Reminiscing about Enoch, that year was full of miracles and ministry. One was around Capalis Beach, Washington. The town was begun by an atheist who forbade anyone to start a

Sunday school. There were plenty of saloons and every home was a shambles; but two brothers persisted. A little girl was saved, grew up, went to teacher's college, married a fine Christian and returned to teach in the school. The atheist went to his place, and the gospel came in.

When we went, there was a pretty, white church, a Sunday school building and parsonage. Every home was now in repair—white picket fences—and at least one Christian living in each home. Only one tavern was left, and it wasn't popular. We had our children's meetings during school time so that we could reach the children who had nothing in two other seaside towns.

Another village was run by a legalistic woman who gave us hospitality. The only missionaries she had a good word for were those who fasted often. Few people came to the Sunday school. She didn't know what to think of our party-like approach, happy choruses and chalk paintings, but people came till the walls bulged. Children were seated on the floor under our feet. They heard the gospel and were being saved. She began to see that God can change the pattern if He likes.

A sinful husband was on his death bed. She told us she had wanted to go and tell him how to be saved, but his wife refused. The wife wanted him to go to hell. I invited this bitter woman to our cookie contest and come-as-you-are program. When she saw Christians could have fun and still be saved, she opened her heart to His life of peace and joy. God changed the heart of the legalistic, long-faced Christian, too.

During the dust-bowl disaster, many from the Midwest had lost everything and migrated to the West to follow the crops or work in mills. Squatters settled along the Columbia River. Sprinkled over the hills were some little farms and many make shift shelters of tin and scrap lumber.

A dear brother from Portland walked those trails to gather a harvest of souls. After years of patient planting, a nice little church was built near the school. He invited us to hold meetings for a month in Shilo Basin. We had a room in the home of one of the Christians who took in foster boys. We would load Enoch with as many as ten to ride the ten miles to the church. Whoever couldn't get in, stood on the running boards.

One of the foster boys was a talented pianist. He had been the bar boy for the priests until he began to sample their liquor. At first, after he was dumped, he would walk for miles to mass; then he learned about the saving grace of Jesus and became a great blessing. The last I heard, he had become a pianist for an evangelist.

One family was part Indian; both parents were alcoholics. The children went to school in rags, hungry and dirty. When we had children's meetings, they came right from school. Their hair, never touched by a comb, was a hunk of matted tangles that I had to cut out so they could even see. As we lovingly cared for them, they began to blossom. The oldest girl earned a New Testament. She cried when she told us that her dad had said it was the work of the devil and burned it.

"Don't worry dear, we'll give you another. Your parents don't understand yet. Keep it in your desk at school till they come to love Jesus."

We spoke at a women's club in Salem and told the ladies of the awful conditions. They sent nice clothing and fruit back with us. On our return, we stopped at a country service station.

"What brings you out in such miserable weather?" a burly, ex-prize fighter asked.

"We're missionaries and are having meetings in Shilo Basin."

"Well, well…what do you know? You ain't got much now at that racket, but if you keep at it you might make a lot of money, like Amy Simple McFerson."

"We're not in it for money," I responded. "God called us to give up all that money could buy. I could have gone back to the entertainment field and made $200 a week, but we chose to go out to serve the Lord by faith. We get fifty dollars a month support. God himself meets all our needs."

He told of preachers and spiritists who had cheated him. "You are not talking about real Christians; they are counterfeits."

We started on—Enoch stopped. "Oh no. This is a fine place to conk out. I just told him the Lord met all our needs, and he says he's an atheist."

The boxer examined the wheel, "A broken axle. You better take my car. I'll gas up. Those yokels up there need something. They're a tough lot. You get one of those kids that have an old junked car like this and bring me the axle, and I'll put it on for you."

"Don't you want some security?" I asked.

"Not for the likes of you! If you can't find one in a couple of days call in for me to get a load of gas."

We drove on praising the Lord. We located an axle. The young man who gave it to us started bringing a string of younger brothers and sisters and they turned to the Lord.

We returned with the axle. He had the car all ready to roll in moments. The church prayed for him and our hostess sent jars of her canned food as gifts, but he said he canned, too. He sent back as many cans of his as she had given.

"It isn't very safe to carry your spare on the front bumper. Here's $10. You go to the junkyard and pick up a luggage rack for the back. I'll put it on." We marveled as we thanked him.

When we got back, we kept praying for the kind, professed atheist.

We had a problem: Each night we would start home loaded and would run out of gas halfway—someone was siphoning gas out of our car. We would get enough from the farm nearby to go on. We'd fill up and run out again the next night. That farmer and several sons needed haircuts, so I cut their hair and invited them to attend our meetings. They did and, before we left, they had a picture taken of the whole family.

"Before you came, the wife and I would leave the kids alone and spend the evenings at the tavern. Now we gather around our dining table and read the Bible and pray. You'll never know how much your coming has meant to us." They gave me the picture to keep.

A young teen lived beyond us and walked the mile to ride with us. Our headlights would get so dim before we got home, the boys guided us with flashlights the rest of the way. "My dad said if I would bring your car on home, he and my brother would re-wire it so the lights wouldn't go out," Jim offered.

He took the car on and we went to bed. Soon we heard voices. We got up to see what was so exciting. Jim, almost in tears, said he had tried the brakes on a hill and the tire on the front bumper fell off and rolled down the hill. He set the hand brake and ran after it, but the car rolled off the road and tipped on its side in the snow. His dad, brother and himself couldn't get it back on the road. Could they borrow a block and tackle? No damage was done to the car. They not only re-wired the electrical system, but they put a tire rack on the back and tightened the brakes.

When we got to town, we got a siphon-proof gas cap so we had no more problem there.

Now we had the ten dollars our atheist friend gave us for a specific purpose, so we went way out of our way to return it. He couldn't imagine anyone doing a thing like that. He filled a gallon jug with oil for a Christmas present. We got cards from him for several years.

We planted; but we must trust the Lord to send others to water and rejoice in the harvest.

CHAPTER 12

Adventure By Conversion

REDDING AND FURTHER IN THE MOUNTAINS... HALLELUJAH!

In Redding, one day, we saw a jeep packed with children. "Where do you live?" we asked.

"In Shingletown."

"Do you have a Sunday school there?"

"What is a Sunday school?"

"It's where people meet to learn about Jesus."

"Who is Jesus?"

"He is God's Son who came to earth to take away our sins; so when we must die, we go on to a beautiful place called Heaven, if we trust Him. Would you like for us to come to your town and tell you more?"

"Oh yes, yes, yes," they all chimed in. "When can you come?"

"We have several other towns first, but as soon as possible we'll come up."

Palo Cedro was next. At the schoolhouse, neighbors agreed to let us come, have story hour for the kids, a women's meeting in the church and an evening family message, each day for two weeks. But who would give us a place to stay?

"If they can put up with what we have, they can sleep in the spare room that has a bed in it and some of the feed," Mrs.

Brush offered. "I'll give them a spot in the fridge, and they can fix their own meals after we go out to milk." When we came to the dairy farm, we thanked them for their hospitality. "We're very busy people, so don't expect to visit with us. Just keep out of our way."

They came to our first evening meeting. Afterward, we went straight to our room. Elizabeth knocked. "Ken has some questions. Would you mind coming out?"

We did. It was midnight before we got in bed.

Next morning at five a.m., there was a knock at our door, "Girls, are you awake? Ken has some more questions he'd like to ask before we go out to milk." The poor cows waited till 8 o'clock to be milked that day. After that, we were with them for meals. Elizabeth brought her grandchildren to the children's meetings and listened with them.

Audrey was giving the story of Cain and Abel. She explained how the innocent lamb was killed for the repentant sinner. The innocent lamb represented the death of the holy Son of God taking the death penalty for the sinner. Abel acknowledged his sin and obeyed God's provision for forgiveness and bringing peace; Cain rebelled against God's plan. He built an altar, admitting he was a sinner, but he offered the works of his own hands. The fruit and vegetables looked pretty, but they came out of a cursed earth—they were lifeless things. God rejected his offerings. Cain got no peace. Sin only increased to the place where he hated his brother and killed him. Cain typified the self-righteous who wanted to go to heaven their own way.

They had felt God was weighing their good works and bad; If the good tipped the scales, they went to heaven; if the bad works were greater, they didn't.

"That was a message for me." Elizabeth went on to explain, "I'm like Cain. I've been trusting in my religious works to save me, but now I realize that only the blood of the Lamb of God can be offered to God for my salvation." She and Ken grew fast in their new-found faith. She drove to another town to get other grandchildren to visit her so she could take them to story hour.

Her daughter was divorced after starting a family of three. She turned and married a divorced man who was a leader in the Communist Party; he had three little ones, too. Grandma was burdened for them.her son lived on the farm with their two little ones. Dianne told Grandma she loved Jesus and she wanted His Bible book of her very own, but she wanted the Jesus words in red. We got her a copy for Grandma to give as a present. She would climb up on Daddy's lap and demand that he read the Jesus words to her.

Then, her daughter's little Duane was stricken with meningitis and not expected to live. Several of the family were in the son's kitchen wringing their hands. Dianne disappeared. When she was missed, they went looking. There she was on her knees by the davenport. She stood up, "It's goin' to be all right. Don't cry. I told Jesus about Duane and He said He will make him well." They went to the hospital. Duane was sitting up wanting his toys—he was healed.

"Don't ever ask me to pray," Elizabeth begged. She had always used a prayer book and never prayed her own prayers.

"Don't worry," I encouraged, "you will. As you get filled with the Spirit, you'll pray out of your heart." The women's meetings kept on going after we left. When we visited later, the women shared the blessings of hearing Elizabeth's prayers.

They were putting all their savings into a search for more water for their dairy herd. After weeks of drilling, all their savings went into a dry hole. "If that had happened to us before you came, we'd have destroyed ourselves. Now that God rules our lives, it is all a part of His plan." Instead of expanding for their son and family, they retired and he kept the dairy. Ken got a job heading the Honor Farm, a halfway house for prisoners. He won the hearts of many of the men; and many, including Indians, were saved. All loved the Brushes.

We went next to a little town, of Oak Run, in the foothills. The Webbers heard Dr. De Haan on the radio, accepted the

Lord and longed for more. An old church had been closed many years. We stayed in the Sunday school room; they brought in cots and a table. We had story hour in the school and the women came to that room for their Bible studies. A little old lady came with a big horn to fit in her ear so she could hear. When I started talking about the precious blood of Jesus shed for our sins, she would remove her hearing aid. That was offensive to her Christian Science training. But, at the end of our stay, I asked her how we are saved. With a sweet smile, she said "By the precious blood of Jesus."

On the last day, the children set out on a treasure hunt that led to the church. We had planned on messages to families. When the children arrived, there were golden ears of corn and a big, potluck feast. When the meeting time came, there sat a whole row of strangers.

Individually, the Lord told us to change our message. While I was laying in the background of the chalk painting, as I did for most of the evening messages, I did an entirely different illustration than planned as Audrey was telling the story of Mel Trotter—the helpless alcoholic—and the terrible things he did to his family in his craving for drink. Try as he would, he had no power. He used the medicine money for his sick baby on drink. She died. He went to the funeral and stole the shoes off of her dead body.

He was cleaning spittoons to get another drink in a saloon. "You're too filthy to live," the bartender shouted. "Why don't you get out and go down to the pier and jump in, you bum!"

As Mel headed for the pier to put an end to his miserable life he passed the Rescue Mission. It was cold and one of the Christians was watching for men who needed to come in. He dragged Mel in, who slumped to the floor in a corner. When his head began to clear, he began to listen. As the love of God began to reach into his heart, he found hope, then faith, then love. He was truly born again and became a new person. The power of alcohol and the bondage to Satan was gone.

We concluded the message the Lord had given us, "Now, I've given you the gospel; we have communicated the Word of

God horizontally. Now it's time for you to do business with God vertically. Right there in your seats you can repent of your sins, confess your need of the Savior and ask Him to come into your heart. He can save you now."

Later, I learned that Dorothy, the wife, had wanted to be saved for years; but when the invitation was given to go to the altar and shake hands with the pastor to get saved, she froze to her seat. That night she trusted Jesus right where she was.

After the meeting, we were introduced to the new family— the brother of the new Christian who wanted us to come. We were invited to their home for fellowship. We learned the family had just arrived from Wilmington, and Paul was looking for work. As we joked and had a casual happy time together, Paul stood off in a corner watching. As we went to the car, Dorothy ran out.

"How did you know?" breathless.

"Know what?" I inquired.

"Did someone tell you Paul was an alcoholic?"

"No one, unless it was God."

"That message was just for us." She explained how he had gone down from high positions to poverty. They were about to lose their home, so they rented it and came in an old wreck of a car to his brother's, who would give him a job on the road crew. They hoped a new environment would give him victory.

We had to go farther into the mountains next day. We met in the little schoolhouse. The families were segregated into blacks and whites who avoided each other.

Before long, the love of Jesus began to dissolve the prejudice. By the end of two weeks, they were of one spirit.

During the depression, a couple took a homestead way back in—inaccessible by road. They started trekking in as real pioneers and built up a log cabin and all the farm buildings before a road was even near. The mother was a Christian and tried to raise her three sons and daughter for the Lord. The oldest was away in school when we came, but she brought her boys to our meetings. They were among those who were born again.

They invited us to their farm. The road was passable in good weather by then, so we went. It was like stepping back into our early history. The venison was frozen on the back porch; nights at that height kept it cold. Hunks were taken off as needed. We just loved those hardy wholesome friends.

Later on, we returned just before our trip to LA to get silver tip spruces for our loved ones' Christmas trees. We parked on the nearest possible road and hiked on in. They didn't think we dared to come in winter. They were delighted and cut a nice load of silver tips and, with a sled, climbed the steep hill to our car. We hadn't gone very far in the dark when our lights went out. The snow was white on the road and the Lord kept us in the center till we came to a village and help.

While we were up at that place, Paul said to his family, "Let's go up and see what the girls have to say." They came again to visit at the next place. He was seeking God.

At last we could make the trip way up to Shingletown. I gave a program at the school and invited everyone to attend the evening meetings there.

"We thought you would never come." the children told us. They were really excited. This mill town was owned by a mother and two sons and their families. They knew their children needed some spiritual guidance, but no one knew how to start.

Nearly everyone in town turned out. By this time, the Lord had provided a little tear-drop trailer, so we had a place to eat or sleep where there wasn't any hospitality offered. As they filed out, no one offered to entertain us…until the last family, "We don't have much to offer you. Our home is so small, but you can park your trailer in our yard and we'll share our food."

We followed them deep into the dark woods. They helped us level the trailer and left us in total darkness. I got our big flashlight and crawled in. I looked at Audrey's legs crusted with red soil that she had picked up on her sweating legs.

"You can't get in bed with those feet. We have running water right beside the trailer. Come on we're going to get clean."

A plank bridged the mountain stream. A good place to wade in was on the other side.

"Come on in, the water's fine." I tried to keep my teeth from chattering.

"Oh...it's too cold, Brr."

"You might as well get it over with."

We heard something on the plank.

"Trip trap, trip trap, who goes over my bridge?" I joked turning the flashlight that way. There was a pretty, black-and-white skunk waving its plume like tail. Fortunately, the little fellow went on up stream.

We went to bed. In the middle of the night, Audrey went outside. A horrible sound nearby made Audrey dive back into the trailer. "You don't get me out of here till morning. What was it?"

"I don't know. It didn't sound like a bear, but it must be big to make such a noise."

Next morning, the family butchered a huge pig. "...But we killed a bear right where your trailer is sitting," they laughed.

The nice home of one son and his family was about a block from the school. She walked over the first night, but a big bear followed her, so she drove the rest of the time. They entertained us several times. They told how they left the door open one day when they went to see his mother. When they got home, a skunk had taken possession of the rocking chair and refused to leave. So they went to stay with Mother. For several days, the intruder enjoyed their home. Then he disappeared, so they came in; but when they looked in the closet, there was the little rascal sound asleep on the pile of dirty clothes on the floor.

They had a cat that would knock on the window when he wanted in. While the husband was reading the paper, he heard the knock. "Come on in, the door's open," he called, not noticing until the eyes looking in raised up and he jumped up. "Oh no, don't come in." It was a big bear. We heard many true stories of experiences with wild life in the mountains.

The husband of this home was an accomplished organist, not at all like the tough, timber men. After his wife saw her need of the Savior, she longed for her husband to join her on the High Way. He promised to attend our last meeting.

Returning from a trip to the valley, he was speeding around a mountain curve. The car went out of control. He was thrown out onto the road as the car flew over into the ravine. A loaded truck coming down did the impossible: It screeched to a stop in the length of the logs, saving our friend from a mutilated death. But his right arm was so crushed, it had to be amputated.

When her husband didn't get home, we went to prayer. God heard. By a miracle, He gave him another chance. "If your hand offends...it's better to enter the Kingdom of Heaven with one arm than to go into Hell with both arms."

We were meeting in a small schoolhouse near Shasta Dam. The memory of a little girl tenderly helping her drunken dad out the door after it was over, is indelible. So many families were in dire poverty because of bondage to liquor.

One couple invited us to park our wee trailer beside their shack. They had no table, so we shared their meager fare, eating off of trays—the rough ends of boards picked up at the mill. Soon, the gospel penetrated their souls. We gave them a Bible. I was tempted to throw out the paperbacks, but decided the Holy Spirit would convict them. Changes took place fast: Billy was the worst boy in school—till he trusted Christ.

"I don't know what you've done to Billy," the woman teacher commented, "but now he's the best one. I've learned more about the Bible in these weeks you've taught the children, than all the years I've gone to the Mormon Church." Wherever the Word was taught, those who believed made productive workers and loving homemakers.

Years later, after I was married, Billy's mother needed to care for her mother for a month or so, and Billy lived with us.

He carried his New Testament in his shirt pocket and read it when he had a chance. His teacher showed a film in class glorifying Mormonism. He forbade Billy to bring his Bible.

When Billy told me, I went to the superintendent. He was a model student, but he refused to conform in that one point. To penalize him, the teacher made him run around the track till he was exhausted. Still, he carried his New Testament. We stuck up for him. He was willing to suffer for Christ's sake.

CHAPTER 13

Appreciating Bible Concepts
WHISKEY TOWN AND IRON MOUNTAIN

Our next two weeks were at Whiskey Town—yes, that's the real name and the real condition, for every shack was destroyed by the demon of drink.

A Christian teacher had come with a heavy burden for the poor, neglected children. School was out for a few days over Thanksgiving, so the tired teacher gave us the keys so she could take a break.

We had never seen such a wild bunch as we did that first day, but before we were finished, two sisters were the only ones who hadn't asked the Lord to come into their hearts. We asked them why as they left the story hour the last day.

"Our father will beat us if we are late."

"Do you want to be saved?"

"Yes, but we live way up the road. We can't fool around—Dad will be mad."

"We'll take you home. We'll explain to him that you want to be saved."

It was quite a hike the girls took each day to go to school. We found the mother had died, and the father was trying to raise his three daughters alone. We explained what we were teaching—the wonderful new life to be had in Christ—and that these two had asked the Lord to save them.

"We're having a play at the schoolhouse tomorrow evening, and your girls are in it. Will you come and bring them?"

"I'd planned on taking them to Redding to a movie tomorrow."

We all begged him to come. That evening the sister who was in high school was there as well. Parents of all the children came. We set up my stage scenery I had used when I was an educational entertainer and gave an imaginary bird hike. It was of birds I'd painted on silk.

The play included all the children on a hike, singing the songs they had learned in the two weeks of meetings.

"I'm so happy and here's the reason why,..." they sang. Dressed like a bum, Mr. Down and Outer with a big black bag marked S-I-N came in.

"Who's happy all the time? There ain't no happiness in this world except a little you get in a drink."

The children told him of victory over sin and a new life of lasting joy.

A girl dressed as a society dame came also, carrying a bag of sin. She blamed the burden on others who kept her in bondage. The children quoted the Bible verses they had learned and had believed; the salvation message that had brought them understanding and light God gave to them.

They knelt before the cross and the load of sin rolled off as they all sang, "Into my heart, into my heart, come into my heart Lord Jesus."

We held a candle-lighting service. One by one, children made a humble confession of their faith in Christ. Some confessed sins and asked forgiveness of those offended. Some parents joined. Tears flowed; the father and the girls were among them.

"I tried to make my girls do right, but I didn't know how," he sobbed.

"If you had told us this could happen in Whiskey Town before you came, we'd have called you liars," they said.

🦢 🦢 🦢

Iron Mountain was next. All vegetation had been killed by the fumes of a smelter. We climbed the reddened mountain. The teacher let us have the children's meeting in the school.

"If you memorize John 3:16, you can have a New Testament," we offered.

"John who?" inquired the daughter of the owner of the mine. None of them had seen a Bible and knew absolutely nothing of the Word of God, so we had to start from zero. They, including the teacher, were like sponges. By the time of our final program, all had made professions of faith. At the candle-lighting service, only two didn't come up, and that was because their parents wouldn't let them. A Sunday school was started that has carried on.

We stayed in the old rickety barracks, ten miles from the community hall where we had our evening meetings. They had never had anything like the new life we were offering. We had our wire recorder for musical accompaniment, and lots of fun things each night. We had a birthday party for "no one knew who," with object lessons and laughter over the one in the audience who had a birthday closest to the date drawn. They got a cupcake, two candles to blow out, a big lollipop and, after the ordinary birthday song, we sang, "Happy Birthday to you. Only one will not do. Born again means salvation. How many have you?"

Then I gave the message from John 3, that all have sinned, even religious Nicodemus. So Jesus had to come and pay the death penalty for us. For God so loved the world that He gave His only Son that whoever believes in Him, shall not perish, but have everlasting life. All must be born again by trusting Jesus as their Savior.

Another evening was a come-as-you-are party, where a prize was given to the one who was there dirt and all. The message was, "Just as I am, without one plea, but that the Savior died for me."

Another time was a cookie contest; and all who brought cookies got first prizes. Heaven is the prize for all believers.

One that was hilarious was aimed at young people: Truth or Consequences. We lined them up and asked simple questions at first, then harder, until some were getting a laugh when they had to do some silly thing. Then the natural clown in the group was asked, "Who was Mephibosheth?" Of course he didn't know, so he had to sit on a high chair wearing a baby cap with a bottle in his hand.

My message was of the love David had for Jonathan, who was in line to become king after Saul died. Jonathan wanted his friend David to have the throne. When a kingdom was taken over by another king, it was customary that all heirs be killed. David had promised he wouldn't kill any of Jonathan's family when he became king. Since Jonathan was killed along with Saul, David soon became king. He searched for the only son left of his friend's family who was hiding in the desert. Mephibosheth was a very frightened, crippled man when he was brought before the powerful King David; but love and grace gave him a place of honor and wealth. My message was how the grace of God brings us out of fear into feasting. If you don't obey the truth, you must suffer the consequences.

The old grandma and her son, who played the fiddle for dances, stayed with the family who gave us their hospitality. The first night as we sat by the fire, Granny piped up, "You say it's wrong to drink a little whisky," she confronted Audrey, defiantly.

"But we didn't say one word about drinking."

"Well, I say it's good for the gout."

We didn't argue, but we did get them to come. Before long, the son was playing our hymns. After meetings were over, many hung around the red-hot, potbelly stove to record songs and hear themselves played back—a novelty in those days.

Loaded with kids each night, we would slide over slippery roads and straddle wash outs, prayerfully.

"That's where Uncle Ezra went over."

"That's the place where my cousin slid off and was killed," we heard.

"My times are in His hands." Through the many dangers we had already experienced, we were confident our lives were indestructible until He was finished using us as we served these needy souls.

Again, the neighbors there said they never would have believed people for miles around would come in the winter cold to the old hall every night, for two weeks, on time, and stay late, still sober. Previously, it was used at Christmas and Easter; they came late and returned late, drunk.

The hump in the floor of the hall made a good teeter-totter with the wooden benches. The road's side of the hall was hooked into the high side, with a steep drop off so you could look through knot holes in the floor and see, beyond the stilts, the valley below. Where we stayed, it was the same. We laughed, "That's where you could stand on the porch and spit a mile!"

The old grandma and her son went into Redding and, as we were leaving, they presented us lovingly with Christmas gifts, "We've decided we must quit drinking and playing for dances, and start going to church."

We promised we would try to come back and help them get Sunday services started, but we never got to. Heavy snows closed roads for a long time. Later the American Sunday School Union took over.

One of the mothers who came to Christ begged us to take her to visit her teenage son who was in juvenile hall awaiting trial. We learned of her husband's death in a mine accident. She became so morbid, her son ran away; in hunger, he stole food and was caught.

"You and Audrey stay in the car. I want to talk to Steve alone for a while," He was a fine-looking kid.

"I suppose you think that nobody loves you now?"

"I don't know why they should."

"You are loved no matter what you have done. First, your mom loves you, Jesus loved you enough to die for you, and now I love you, too." I gave him a hug and explained the gospel. In simple, childlike fashion, he opened his heart and the new boy responded through his tears with redemptive relief.

We went to share his joy with his mother. She was happy as they hugged each other with tears of emotion, "I wish I could give you a Christmas present, Steve, but I spent every cent on trying to get you out of this place."

"You have already given me the most wonderful gift in all the world. You've given me my Savior. No money can buy so precious a gift as that!"

I went to the authorities to see if there was some way he could be released.

"He isn't a bad boy. He just couldn't stand being around his mother's grief. He stole to survive."

"If anyone would take him in, he need not go to the reform school. The only other place open to him is a Catholic place and that's no better, his mother doesn't agree to send him there. He can't go to her till she snaps out of it."

I couldn't find a Christian who was willing to give this teen a chance, so he had to go to the reform school, where tough kids usually learn to be tougher. But, Steven soon was returned to the mother, both of them on the highway to Heaven with joy that reached out to the Iron Mountain community.

CHAPTER 14

A Blessed Car
SAMUAL— GOD'S PROVISION

We started to LA for our month off for Christmas. After our little '29 Chevy, Enoch, broke down, the Lord provided a Graham Page 4-door. Because the company had gone bankrupt, parts were hard to get; that's why we got it for so little, but it was high powered and way ahead of other cars for speed and economy. We were thankful. We named that one Samuel, for it was "asked of God"...the perfect answer. You wouldn't believe the roads we traveled and the numbers of people who crowded into it that year.

We were between Tulare and Bakersfield when there was an explosion. The six tires were all right. I opened the hood; a spark plug had blown out of the head. "Lord, what do we do now?" We had learned that every time we were stopped, it was an appointment of the Lord.

Two men, one black and one white, came out of the cotton field. Seeing the trouble, the white man, Truman, said they'd help get the trailer off the highway. "It will sound like a threshing machine, but we could drive to Porterville and knock the head, re-thread the plug hole and put in a larger one." Audrey and Joe guarded the trailer. On the thirty miles to Porterville, I talked about the Lord, how He was with us and how He had sent these men to help us.

We got the extra tools needed and went to work. We got the supercharger off, but the aluminum head refused to budge. It was getting dark. "I'm worried about leaving Audrey there alone with the black man," I expressed my concern. "Oh, he's a Christian, ma'am. He won't hurt her none." I was relieved.

"We better lock the tools inside and try to get back to them, though." We were both hungry, and all the money I had bought one hamburger, which we split.

We started walking. In the dark, a coupe stopped and we climbed in. The man was a Mexican migrant. I started telling him about the Lord as I always did. He began praising the Lord for letting him help a missionary. "I just accepted the Lord in some revival meeting the other day," he grinned.

"Where do you want me to take you?"

Pulling up along the sleeping trailer, we found no one. Coals were still glowing. They couldn't have been gone long. My flashlight showed a note on the door:

> We are worried about you. I'll try to find a way to
> get to Porterville to look for you.

We went to the circle of shacks for migrant workers where Truman lived. Praise the Lord, Audrey was still there.

One of the men would take his car to pull the trailer there if we would put gas in. We went in the shack and huddled close to a tin wood stove while the two men went to bring the trailer. The one room had a double bed, a cot, a kitchen table and a couple of old chairs. Truman's mom was in bed and his brother was on the cot with a thin mattress for a cover. With the slurred voice of a man intoxicated, he roused to say, "If'n you all are cold, ya can crawl in with ma."

We did. But Ma chewed snuff and had to aim at a tin can now and then. Besides, she had the itch, so we didn't sleep.

Toward morning, the men unhitched the trailer in front of the door. We got busy using our equipment and food supply to feed the men. The all-purpose pan they had didn't look inviting.

The next morning, it was pouring. No cotton picking that day, so all the men filled the cabin and we gave them stories of the transformed lives we had seen and the power of God to do the same for them. The black Joe came with his car, and we went to Porterville to pull our Samuel to the cabin. I learned that Truman and his friend had just gotten out of the penitentiary. They were worried—but I wasn't. I was perfectly confident the Lord was in control of the whole situation.

One of the men went to find his cousin. He had gotten saved in a Pentecostal meeting once and was going strong for a while; but then he failed and "lost his salvation and was back in the world."

"If you can pay for the gas, I'll take you to LA," he promised.

We piled the Christmas trees in and most-needed luggage, locking the rest in the trailer. Truman thought he could fix the car, so I sold it to him for seventy-five dollars.

Juanita named "The Bird Girl" for ten years as an educational entertainer

*Juanita and her
husband Bissell*

*During family devotions,
Alex and Jimmy loved to sit
on Bissell's lap*

Bissell and the boys on the beach in Arklow.

The children after Sunday services in Avoca.

Celebrating birthdays at the Baby home.

God used an old clay vessel in needy places around the world.

CHAPTER 15

A Blessed Christmas
ISAAC— GOD'S PROVISION

Our December support of fifty dollars each and our Christmas gifts were not much to offer for another car. We went out to Wilmington to visit Paul and Dorothy Webber.

It was over a year since they heard the gospel in the little old brown church, and they had visited other places we were serving.

We had gone back to see them and his brother and family when we came back from Los Angeles, Dorothy ran into my arms, "Oh, I'm so glad you came. I was just praying and praying you'd come back. Paul is in deep trouble. He said he wanted to be saved, but he had to clean up first. He stayed away from alcohol for a whole month. He was doing fine on his brother's road crew.

"Then, one of the men enticed him to just take a swig. He couldn't stop. He got drunk, got in a company truck and headed down the road. His brother chased after him. He ran off the bridge and wrecked the truck. He was thrown from it onto bushes so he badly wasn't hurt. His brother carried him home. When he came to, he was so ashamed he wanted to die. Wayne hugged him, 'We love you Paul, no matter what you've done, and God loves you too.'

"That night, Paul paced the floor. He had tried and failed. I had told him to come to Jesus just as he was. He could give him the power. That night he surrendered. Only God could overcome the demon of drink that enslaved him.

"Wayne had to fire him from the road crew, but recommended him for another job, now that he was saved."

Audrey and I were a week into the hardest community yet. We were the guests of a couple who followed rank, modernist teachings. That Saturday, here came Paul and Dorothy with their three children. "We're on our way home," they rejoiced. "Now that we are all trusting in Jesus, we know He will help us live victoriously."

The Lord used that visit to encourage us. The last week, God broke through the opposition.

Now back to our visit in their home in Wilmington: Dorothy led us to the kitchen. She flung open the door of the fridge. "Look," she boasted, "it's full of food. Before it was beer and wine and whisky. Now we are a happy family."

Paul was a skilled and intelligent man, holding a fine job, till drink took control. From being a popular Mason and holding a fine position, he had lost everything. Now he had a good job and didn't return to Masonry but Paul took us to a Mason friend who sold used cars.

After showing us several beyond our price, the friend said, "This Dodge just came in. It hasn't been checked or cleaned up." He named the price he had paid for it: two cents less than we had.

"Anyone who would do for Paul what you girls have done, deserves a break. You can take the car and if anything goes wrong with it while you are around, I'll fix it for free."

We named that car Isaac—it had a ram on the radiator. As Isaac was offered for sin, so this car was to be offered for sin. It was a sturdy workhorse that would carry us over icy mountain roads the next year.

🐏 🐏 🐏

Returning to the field, we went to see Truman. The tools had been stolen. Someone had tried to force the lock on the trailer door. The window on the other side would have slid open easily, but God didn't let them.

They wanted us to go to Woodville and have meetings. The road to Iron Mountain was closed, so we had two weeks in the little town. Friendships that have remained all these years were established.

Hugh and Hazel Honneycutt ran a hardware and post office. He gave me the necessary tools. Later, a widow sold her husband's tools for ten dollars, and I had far more than we had lost. Truman came, but I don't know whether he was ever saved. He was another alcoholic.

The Lord gave me the talent and joy I get when using my oil paints. I did a very large picture of a peaceful pond for their baptistery. It looked so real you expected a fish to surface. People went up to see if it was three-dimensional.

Bev and Helen Jackson were discouraged. They were in Fernwood, Idaho, under Village Missions. One of the influential women swore she would drive them out. She had the general store and post office. Most folks charge for groceries so they owed her money, and it was important to keep on friendly terms. When the Jacksons sent out letters inviting folks to attend special meetings, she would hold them until after the date planned and then mail them. She lived right next to the old church. Bev and Helen parked their mobile home in back of it and almost single-handedly put up the framework for a parsonage. They had been invited to come by the tavern owner.

The old church had been put up for sale and a competitor wanted to buy it for another tavern. "It wouldn't be right to turn a church into a tavern," he insisted.

The women were meeting in Santa, a nearby village, and we were invited to offer our program. "What shall we do to open this door?" I prayed.

"Offer them handicrafts to draw them in."

After an hour of hemming and hawing over little things, they introduced us. Almost choking from the cigarette smoke, I offered to teach them handicrafts, and a Bible study for two weeks, a story hour for the kids and evening meetings for the families. Before folks were enslaved to television, anything new and interesting that was offered was a welcome diversion from their drab lives.

They all turned out for the crafts and loved it. Then I opened up my illustrated study of the plan of God for the ages. If they came once, they were hooked. They didn't want to miss a class. After a couple of days, I'd hear them say, "I can't stay for the whole morning tomorrow, but I don't want to miss that Bible study."

News spread to Fernwood. We were invited there and many of the women from Santa wanted to keep on coming all the way there.

We were staying with the Jacksons. Ike was one of the young men who had been converted through the ministry of Bev when he was at Emida. He came to visit the Jacksons and a lasting friendship resulted. It was time for them to leave us to carry on our meetings while they went to California for a visit with friends and relatives, and to raise support and rest.

Winter comes early in the mountains. The Lord opened the hearts of several. One family invited us to go to St. Mary's to shop for Christmas. I begged to stay to catch up on preparations, so Ike and Audrey had a good visit. They hadn't been gone long when the lights went out and the fan that circulated heat, stopped. I crawled under the covers. We were used to outages. Power was still off the next day. Everyone else had electricity. We checked the fuse box in the home of our opponent next door.

"The girls were using so much power the box got red hot," she lied. "So I threw the switch. Now if you want lights, you'll have to pay for transferring the meter and all over to the church." That was a costly change we couldn't afford. We had propane and could cook, but the water froze. It could be hot halfway up in the air and freeze a bucket of water on the floor. When we were up, we kept on the go to keep our feet from freezing, but we didn't complain.

Mr. Dahl came by from his tavern to see how we were doing. When he saw the situation, he shook his head. "We have a spare bedroom and it's warm there. If you don't mind, the wife and I would love to have you come on over."

We did. They had perhaps the nicest house in town. Audrey had a lovely singing voice and Mr. Dahl could play the piano. They began singing many of the old hymns. He had drifted far away from some godly training, it seemed.

We had been training Ike to do the work of a deacon and decided it was time to serve communion. We insisted that a man should conduct it. With tutoring, he was ready. The believers came. I felt impelled to invite the Dahls; perhaps they were backslidden believers. I donned my warm coveralls to walk the icy distance.

"Would you like to join us for the communion service?" I asked. "It is for anyone who has put their trust in the shed blood of the Lord Jesus."

"I'd just love to go," Mrs. Dahl responded, "but with my husband being in the tavern, they would think we were hypocrites."

"No, dear, they wouldn't. The few who are there are all sinners saved by the grace of Jesus. Would you like to come, too, Mr. Dahl? You can if you've trusted Christ."

"I tried once but I couldn't hold out."

"If you knew an orphan boy you loved a lot and saw he was headed for disaster, and you wanted to adopt him so you could be a dad to guide him, you couldn't make him love you and be your son, could you?"

"No, he would have to be willing."

"Well, say he was anxious to have a home, a dad to love and guide him to maturity; so the adoption went through and you brought him home. Would you say, 'Now that you are my son, you must keep all my rules or out you go?'"

He shook his head.

"Do you think you're better than God?" I shot back. "No, you would nurture him with loving patience and so live before him that he would want to live like you. That's the way our Heavenly Father is: He adopts us if we are willing; then we become His children. We begin to love Him because He first loved us and gave Himself for us. Because we love Him, we strive to do His will; and as we do, we become more and more like Him."

He walked over to the window and gazed at the white snow a long time, in deep meditation. Slowly, he turned around and, scarcely conscious of our presence, he left the room.

His little wife rushed into my arms sobbing, "That's just what he needed!" The last I heard of Mr. Dahl, he was going from church to church in a ministry of music; the tavern was closed.

On the last day was our big final program with the play that included all the children. We were invited to have a meal with dear farm folks just across the river. The first ice storm left the roads slick; we had to go slow over the icy bridge. A sharp right angle led up the hill skirting the rushing mountain torrent below. I got halfway to the top when we began to slide back. I set the brakes and jumped out, hoping I could push on a rock and make the car slide down on the other side.

Slamming the door and pushing, I saved the car from going over the edge; but I went over a sixty-five foot drop to the icy river and came to a stop with one foot in the water.

"Nita, Nita," Audrey screamed in the darkness. The little boy with us was also hysterical.

"I'm all right, Audrey." I climbed up the rocky bank. The car had stopped, balanced on a culvert.

We hiked on up to the farm. The man took a look at the car. It had to stay balanced between the road and the river till the log-loading truck came and lifted it off the next day.

We went on with the meeting as planned. No one knew I was in pain. Fortunately, the Jacksons had given me a fur liner for my thin coat. The extra padding had kept me from a broken back.

The next day, I tried to direct the packing in order to start meetings the next week at Emida. Muscular spasms forced me to admit the suffering. They took me to the hospital in St. Mary's. X-rays showed cracked ribs and vertebra, so I was put in a straight jacket and sent to bed for a month. We had to postpone the meetings, and we were given hospitality for two weeks.

The bar maid was one of the many who visited me. One by one, beside my bed the Lord brought them. Even the one who had caused such heartache was changed when I volunteered to teach her how to make the beautiful wagon-wheel rugs the others made. As we left for Montana, the ex-bar maid brought us a big box of food. She was out of a job, but God had a better one waiting.

Our ministry in Fernwood was completed. The Jacksons returned to a more loving group. I couldn't stay in bed, although the healing was not complete; we were called up into Montana.

CHAPTER 16

Accepting By Choice
Montana, Audrey and Ike

In August, after our conference in Seattle, we had headed for Lincoln, Nebraska, with Mother, Doris and a Chinese friend from Biola. They had never seen Glacier, Yellowstone and the Tetons so, after the thrill of seeing God's great handiwork, we put the girls on a bus for Biola and we went on to Lincoln, Nebraska.

Staying overnight in a state park, we enjoyed a friendly rest and shared some of the stories of lives changed by the Spirit of God with a ranger.

"I wish you'd come to Montana. There are so many towns without a church or Sunday school," he explained. "In the required courses on the history of Montana, they said it was one state that had been spared evangelical preaching."

He gave us a donation and asked us to pray. We did, never dreaming it would be us the Lord would send.

His gift met our need to reach Lincoln. My sister's children were half grown. We promised I'd give the bird hike program if they got a group of kids to meet in their big yard. Several mothers joined them, and we gave them the gospel as well with favorite object lessons. That night, when the children were sent to bed, I followed them and each one asked Jesus to come into their hearts. The seed was planted. As the years brought maturity, Dan made his decision public in Youth for Christ and married a lovely, dedicated wife. They are now missionaries with Masters Mission, training new ones in practical skills before they meet hardships on the field.

After I was married and we were involved in Hume Lake Christian Conferences for four months each summer, Marie spent some summers with us and grew like a weed. Then her sister, Louise, came. "I just had to come back," one of them expressed her feelings. "I was starved. They don't preach there like they do here."

They didn't realize it wasn't the location, but the theology. Liberal churches teach that the Bible contains the Word, but you don't take it too seriously. They think science proves there are errors. The Evangelicals take God's Word as true from cover to cover; and we are to believe it, properly study it as His story and obey the Author.

My brother-in-law filled the tank and checked the car before we started back. We stopped to visit Marie in Kansas. Then, as we went through the Indian reservation, we saw a little building: The Good News Mission.

"That looks like the real thing," I told Audrey. "Let's turn around and see."

A middle-aged lady greeted and welcomed us to come in.

"You look sick," I noticed. "We'll come in and eat lunch with you if you go to bed and let us prepare it." She complied. We looked through the kitchen. The cupboards were bare. Our trailer was well stocked with cans given to us at a food shower. We hadn't needed much of it, so we unloaded and prepared a good meal. We learned that her husband and Navajo Bible teacher had recently died. Her adopted Navajo son was away at school. The little Indians she kept were in local school and would soon come home hungry. That was the lowest time of despair she had ever had. Then the Lord gave us the privilege of being led to be His answer to her need.

Years later, my husband and I visited her. God had blessed. Her son was married and leading the mission, an Indian ministering to his own people.

We went on to Los Angeles. We were hurrying to reach Audrey's home while her brother was visiting, but he had just left. We were praying for him. As a child, he had signed a little Gideon New Testament, but any faith he might have had was destroyed as he climbed the ladder of higher education. Now, as the leading professor of history, he was given the commission to write part of F. D. Roosevelt's life and was given access to his private papers in Hyde Park.

"I've never, in all my life, seen anyone as bitter as your brother was when he learned what was going on behind the scenes. He was sworn to secrecy, so he couldn't tell me more," she told us.

When I spent over a year in Washington DC near the White House and saw their close fraternizing with Communists, I was not surprised.

Let's return to our call to Montana. The young couple had almost single-handedly built a lovely church with parsonage attached. He had financed it by working in the mill.

They gave and gave—picking up children, treating them to sleigh rides and all sorts of enticements—and they got only "Rice Christians," our term for those who profess to be Christians for material gain. They were ready to give up. They contacted our mission, "You can have it if you'll send someone to carry on." They left and we were sent.

Ike offered to drive halfway from Fernwood as he planned to visit his sister. He cried as we saw him board his bus. He placed a big kiss on my cheek. Then he kissed Audrey on the lips, then another, and he escaped into the bus. He wrote that he had planned to witness, but he cried all the way so he didn't think he would be a good example of a happy Christian.

We learned that when the school in Trego had burned down, the church was used till the new one was built with the promise the pump at the school would furnish water for the church. But, when we came, they shut off the water so only a drip came through. Chopping a hole in the ice down on the river or melting snow added to the accumulated drips we caught.

The furnace below was made of two oil drums welded together. The logs to feed it were the length of the drums and up a hill. They had to be hauled daily on a wheelbarrow. The generator was temperamental; it would refuse to start. When we had special evening meetings, I'd have to beg help from neighbor men.

"What does your mission mean by sending a couple of women here in the dead of winter?" someone asked.

"God knew what He was doing. If a man was along, the man was expected to do it all, just like the discouraged couple had learned."

As men came to help, they got acquainted and gradually got involved.

Communism was being taught in the school. That's about all they were taught. Teachers were late so the kids ran wild. Teachers sat with feet propped up on their desks and their cigarette butts cluttered the floor. They tried every way to keep the children from coming over for the children's meetings at noon or recess.

Since we couldn't train the children for the Easter program, we used my string puppets to tell the story.

Over icy roads, I would go one way for a couple of hours picking up children; while Audrey taught them, as I'd go the other way. We had no heater in the car and it was sub-zero most of the time. I had to keep scraping a peep hole through the ice on the windshield. After my experience on the ice in Idaho, we got recapped snow tires that had sawdust or nut shells in the tread. As the tires wear down, particles of sawdust or nut shells would fall out and renew the traction. Where many cars were in the ditch, ours managed to stay in the track—usually.

One night, a farmer friend came asking if we had any milk. Twin babies were starving. Fortunately, friends let us buy several cases of food wholesale to take with us. We gave him a case of canned milk.

We heard how the father had been cheated out of his share of a dairy by a crooked partner. A job was offered up there, so he brought his family; but then he learned how crooked the man who wanted him was and he refused to submit to his demands. As newcomers, they couldn't get welfare. When our farmer friend saw there was no smoke coming from their house, he found all of the family in bed to keep from freezing and the cupboards empty. They would soon be dead. Our friend shot a deer and brought wood, but the twin babies needed milk. We were able to supply.

One day, the little girl came with a pan of homemade biscuits her mother made as a thank you gift. As soon as they had warm clothing, they were regular members of church. When they got welfare, they had warm boots and coats.

Then we got a letter from Czechoslovakia telling of a sick son and their great need for warm clothing. We responded with a box. Guess who gave; they gave their new boots and coats. They could get by with their old ones. It wouldn't be worth the postage, they said, to send their old ones. How dear this family was.

We challenged the men to be the leaders in the church and the spiritual head of their family.

We had a party for the young people. There were fun things, but also a devotional message. A high-school boy was touched. He made an appointment to meet us where no one would see us talking. His Catholic parents wouldn't let him come to meetings, but he was starved to hear more. He'd hide under the hay to read his Bible.

On the bus, he was nicknamed Preacher's Boy. One day the bus broke down in Eureka, right near the Baptist minister's home. He got permission to run over to see him.

"Has so and so been saved yet?" he asked.

"Yes." the young pastor told of several of his friends who had been saved. Going over the list of kids he was praying for, he named others who were near.

He was to give a report on his favorite book; he preached a sermon to the class. The teacher stopped him before he gave an invitation. He was valedictorian, so he gave his message to honor the Lord.

He wanted to attend Biola and sent for an application, but his parents confiscated his mail so he didn't know whether or not he had been accepted. All summer he manned a forest tower and memorized scriptures. All the towers were hooked up by radio—each man could choose a favorite program, but all had to listen. He chose dear Dr. Fuller of the Old Fashioned Revival Hour. On Neil's last day on duty, he preached to all the rest. He sent out an SOS to his Christian friends. His parents threatened to put him in an insane asylum if he went to Biola. Hitchhiking from the Canadian border to LA, spending nothing for food, he hoped he had been accepted and had enough for tuition and all needs. He was enrolled.

Later, his mother said if he was that determined, she'd let things go. I visited him once at Biola. He was still soaking up all he could get. Later, he visited us after I was married. He went on into the ministry and part of his family had come to the saving faith.

We had a sudden thaw. Melted snow flooded down the hill, washing away part of the foundation. A stream flowed through the furnace room and out the door on down to the river. Suddenly, the temperature dropped and the waterfall and stream became ice. Chopping away the ice to get the door open and hauling logs down to feed the fire was no small task.

Then, one cold night, drunken teens began pelting the church and parsonage with large stones, leaving dents in the wooden siding and a big broken window in our bedroom. Our flannelgraph board covered the area. The Lord held our insurance policy, so we had no fear of those determined to drive us out.

One day, a letter came from Ike. Sometimes it was to Audrey and me; this time, it was only her. I had observed an increasing interest. I called to Audrey, "You got a letter." She went inside and I busied myself shoveling snow. She came to the door, "Nita, Nita, what is this?"

"You tell me."

"It looks...it looks...like...a proposal!" overcome with emotion. "What shall I tell him? You know my folks would never accept him. They'd call him a country hick," she cried. "He's been hurt already so much, I couldn't add any more sorrow."

"Don't you think the Lord can do the leading and healing? Isn't he Ike's Lord as well as yours?"

"What shall I tell him?"

"You go into the bedroom and pray and seek God's will for your lives. I'll do all the work. You wait on the Lord until you are sure, and then write down what is in your heart."

He had written that he wanted to come up right away if she said yes, to give her a ring.

"One thing to tell him for sure: He is not to come for two weeks. We're moving to another village fifty miles north, and there's no place for him to stay there."

She had me read and approve her letter, closing with, "I love you very much."

When her letter reached him, he was afraid to open it for fear she'd say no. When he did, he rushed to the jeweler, "I want a diamond ring."

"What size?"

"Oh, I don't know. She has slender fingers."

"I'll loan you this set of sizes. You see which one fits and I'll send you the right size when you send these back."

As fast as his little old car would travel, he headed for Trego.

Saturday evening, he knocked on our door. "Ike, you rascal! I told you not to come for two weeks."

"I couldn't wait. I have to see which ring fits her so I can get the right size."

"Well, come in out of the cold. This causes complications. I'll leave you alone to make sure you are in the Lord's will. Then, if you are sure, I must announce your engagement in the services tomorrow and arrange for someone to give you a place to stay."

Because his radiator leaked he didn't have antifreeze in it. When he went out, the water had frozen and cracked the block; so then he couldn't leave—a good excuse to stick around, but a heap of extra work for me. It meant we had to drive fifty miles over icy mountain roads, each way, each day. A farm family took Ike in, and we continued staying in the parsonage and holding Sunday services.

Then our brakes went out and we had to wait for parts to be mailed in. Ike mailed the rings and her size and waited for the diamond to be returned for an engagement party. So, for two weeks, Ike drove our car using gears instead of brakes to go to our meetings.

One enemy was the county superintendent. She sent out a notice to all her schools to forbid us using any public schools to propagate our dangerous teachings. She claimed we were bringing in rabies to kill the dogs and children.

"How ridiculous can she get," some of the men complained and spoke in our behalf. We wanted to meet her and clear our name, so one weekend we went. The short route was a narrow road on a ledge along the river. A thaw had made the road deep mud. We careened back and forth between the rock wall and the drop off, pulling back inches from the edge. Way below was the icy water of the most beautiful color on earth, but I didn't relish the thought we might have it for our grave.

God was with us.

When we entered the superintendent's office, she ordered us to get out or she would call the police.

"But we've risked our lives to come and tell you the truth. Please listen," I pleaded.

She went to the phone. A burly policeman came and ushered us out into the hall.

"Look, mister, we risked our lives coming over that river road to clear our name. We have been falsely accused and condemned without a cause. I don't want to go back without someone hearing our side."

"I know you're right," he said sheepishly. "And I believe you, but we have to live in this building with her. Understand?"

She had filled a vacancy, unelected; and when the men we had been ministering to went up in arms, she went out the door.

A dear chiropractor brother-in-Christ, and his lovely wife, in Eureka welcomed us when we could stop on our way. We were exhausted by the time we took the long way back. It was full of potholes and stretches where the frost had thawed beneath the black top. You could stand in the middle and rock the whole road. If you went over these places fast it was all right; but if it broke through or someone had dropped in, you were in trouble. Three tires were ruined by those potholes.

When the doctor gave us a massage and treatment one day, a refugee was in his home. Their church had sponsored her. She listened to my tales of woe with a smile, then with a saintly satisfaction she commented, "Dot is very goot. When all is easy, no fruit. When much persecution, much fruit." She knew!

As we headed south, snow was banked twenty feet on the sides of the road, and lakes were still frozen near Glacier National Park. It didn't seem like spring. There was much to do to prepare for Audrey's wedding. We spoke at the Christian Business and Professional Women's Club dinners and prayer groups. The one in LA was especially responsible for upholding us.

CHAPTER 17

Audrey Becomes Called

The three years Audrey and I were teamed up under Youth Home Mission were so full and so rewarding, we had no desire for anything better. There were dangers and opposition, but we knew we were indestructible under His wing.

God had other plans beyond our imagination. When Audrey became Mrs. Vernon Badget, she didn't toss her bouquet—she came down from the platform and plunked it in my lap.

"Here, you take this."

"That's not for me," I laughed. "I wouldn't marry any man that didn't put the Lord first in his life, and there aren't any of that kind who aren't already taken."

"God can do anything. Look what He's done for me. We're praying you'll have the same kind of happiness."

"No way. I'm too old."

The full days of preparing for her wedding, and the packing of Mother's belongings after the funeral of the lady who had cared for her, took every ounce of strength. Since no one else would take care of her, I had to take her with me. With Audrey and I each receiving fifty dollars a month support, plus faith, we never had a penny too much or too little. Could I trust the Lord to meet the needs of my mother and all other expenses with only one fifty-dollar check?

It was ten o'clock by the time we reached Fresno, 230 miles north. I was so tired, I couldn't remember the name or location of the friend who had opened her home to us before.

"Call Mrs. Shearer," the Lord reminded me of her invitation to stay with her anytime.

"Yes, I'm still up. Come on. Will you teach my Sunday school class tomorrow?" I was glad to.

But when she welcomed us, she saw how very weary I was. "No, you go right to bed. You need rest more than church tomorrow."

After a delicious dinner, a man and a family came in the back door. "Do you remember this gentleman?" she asked. "He's the one who has been paying some of your bills."

I had met Bissell Garrett once at the Fresno Bible House when we stopped for needed supplies. Many of the areas we were in, you couldn't even find a New Testament in a radius of a hundred miles. As we left, he donated boxes of books for children and young people. He'd asked about our mission as he loaded the boxes. Then, when we ran out, we sent for supplies and told how valuable the books were. The mail brought our order paid in full by Mr. Garrett. Now I was able to thank him personally.

Mrs. Shearer ushered Mother and the farm family he came with into the living room and left us standing by the back door. He had a keen interest in all the recent happenings.

As I narrated the narrow escapes we experienced in the mountains of Idaho and Montana, tears ran down his cheeks.

There's one man who has a real passion for souls, I thought. Over an hour slipped by as if a moment.

"If we're going to get chores done in time to attend church, we better go." the farmer called.

As Bissell got in the back seat, the Lord spoke to me as clearly as a human voice, "That's going to be your next partner."

I nearly fell over. I had prayed a lot for one, but I expected a lady. I looked at him. "Could I love him as a wife should love her husband?" The voice inside: I suppose I could, if the Lord did it.

I turned around; Mrs. Shearer was standing in the doorway. "Juanita, have you ever considered marriage?"

I nearly fell over again.

"I came near to marrying a professing Christian. I was so thankful the Lord protected me from making such an awful mistake, I swore I'd never again take one step toward marriage. I wouldn't marry any man that didn't put the Lord first.

"Bissell Garrett is that man," she exclaimed. "I've felt for a long time that you two belonged together. He has refused to marry anyone who isn't totally sold out to the Lord." She sat down and told of his many wonderful ministries.

"If this is really the Lord's leading, He will have to do it all. I won't touch it."

I drove on up to Sacramento to enlist Lucille Hutchinson as my helper for VBS at Rescue. Their twins were in their twenties, but mentally retarded. Mother and the twins were an added test, beyond days full of gathering children, teaching lessons and crafts. I'd rush through things each day and pray most of the night.

Tears of exhaustion flowed. "Lord, I can't keep on much longer. If Mr. Garrett would ask me to marry him, it wouldn't be fair to any man at his age to adjust to a wife and assume the care of my mother as well. If this is because of my need, I don't want it."

For several summers, Audrey and I had been given two weeks off to be counselors and craft teachers at Hume Lake Christian Camps. One year, the letter asking us to come was forwarded so often, we were already committed to holding a VBS so we couldn't do it. After Audrey married, the director made sure I was invited early.

Knowing that Bissell was one of six who founded and built up that hallowed spot and was one of the directors, I was especially anxious to go. I wrote HQ for permission and waited. No word came.

"It looks like the Lord has closed the door for me to go to Hume Lake, so I'll offer VBS to the Cool Village." We held

Sunday school and church in Rescue in the morning and drove thirty-five miles to Cool for evenings. I had been stimulating an interest there.

"You can have this vacation Bible school for the next two weeks."

"No, we can't. We're using the Grange Hall. They gave us permission to use it only on Sunday evenings. They won't meet till the end of the month; then we can ask permission to hold VBS."

Back at the little ranch where we stayed, I told Lucille, "It looks like the Lord wants me to go to Hume Lake even without permission from HQ. If I can get the three boys who came to Christ last week to go with us, I'll know it's His will." They had been expelled from school and were living with delinquent parents. They needed to be well-grounded in their new faith. By Wednesday, I had the boys and their tuition pledged. That evening a letter from HQ arrived with permission to go.

Friday was the big program that included all the children in a play. Taverns closed. Everyone came.

Saturday was full of packing, cleaning, getting ready to leave. Lucille's husband was to bring a luggage rack to put on top of my car for bedrolls; but, he forgot. My little sleeping trailer was broken, so, before dawn, I was under my trailer making the necessary repairs. Then I got dressed, picked up a carload of kids, taught the combined Sunday school and church service, closed up the ranch we had used, picked up the boys and held Sunday school and church services at Cool. By ten that night, we were on our way to Hume. We arrived at nine in the morning.

CHAPTER 18

Arranged By Christ

An unexpected suprise for Birdie

"Can you take on a cabin full of girls besides teaching handicrafts?" the director asked.

"Not this week. I've had little or no sleep for days."

They gave Mother and me a nice room in the lodge.

All week I slept when I wasn't teaching crafts. Friday night, I told the Lord, "Maybe this was just a pipe dream because of my desire for a home and love. I'm ready to go back to the field alone, even if it kills me—I know it will with the care of Mother, too."

Saturday morning, I went down to breakfast. Bissell Garrett came hurrying to meet me. "I didn't know you were here. Last word to Mrs. Shearer said you weren't coming. Don and I've been putting up another hall for the young people, so we can run two camps at the same time. We were working against a deadline. Do you want to see it?" We forgot breakfast.

After rejoicing that the hall was ready for the big influx Monday, "Now would you like to see the cabin?" He took my arm up the hill to the back door. "I gathered the stones for the fireplace from many places. Just got it finished."

The bedroom was complete with knotty pine.

"Do you have any suggestions on how to finish the rest?"

I had the feeling this was to be my home. Like the final act of a play, we were actors being directed by our Director.

Two rocking chairs faced a plate glass door that opened to a beautiful mountain scene. We sat there. Bissell bowed his head, "Lord, we don't want to go before you, nor we don't want to lag behind. But we want your will for our lives."

I prayed briefly.

"I must leave right away to get to the men's prayer group I lead. May I see you Tuesday?"

A friend took care of Mother when he came Tuesday. He explained, "Dick Hillis is sick, so he won't be speaking this evening. What would you like to do?"

"Whatever you would like."

We climbed the switchback roads to Inspiration Point. We sat at the base of a Redwood tree and marveled at the grandeur. The lake was a perfect mirror for the colorful Kings Canyon, with the framing of green in the foreground—a picture-postcard scene.

"I suppose you know what I have on my heart," he began. "But I'm quite a bit older than you."

"I know. Mrs. Shearer told me. But if God is in this, that doesn't matter."

He told me how the Lord had spoken to him at exactly the same time the Lord had spoken to me, saying I was the one he had been praying for. He put the Lord first in all things and wasn't willing to compromise.

Meeting me was unique.

The farm family had invited him to their home so often and he had other plans, but this time he felt they would be hurt if he refused. Instead of taking him to their home, they suggested a Chinese dinner in Fresno.

"Would you mind stopping by Mrs. Shearer's?" Bissell suggested. "It would take only a minute, but would save me many miles. I promised to pick up some curtain rods to take to Hame Lake for her cabin." He was there over an hour.

He argued with the Lord all the way to the ranch, "She wouldn't be interested in me. She's a missionary and I'm just a farmer. She's had lots of higher education. I've only finished high school; and she's much younger," he reasoned. Still, when he got his car, he turned around and came back—he'd forgotten the curtain rods. He wanted an excuse to see me again, but I had just headed back to northern California to start VBS.

Mrs. Shearer told him about me.

"You haven't told me one thing I don't already know about that girl." Mrs. Shearer had told me this and that was what made me hold on to my dream.

It seemed only minutes up there as we wept for joy, as we saw His plan unfold to us as a team.

"I have a cabin full of teens this week. We better get back or I'll be having to answer a lot of questions."

"Nine o'clock." We checked his watch in the moonlight. "They'll just be getting out of the meeting."

As I got out of the car, the grounds were vacant. That was strange.

"If we announce our engagement at the banquet on Friday, we better get the rings tomorrow." Bissell suggested.

That came as a shock. Things were happening too fast. "If that's what you want, OK. We can go after handicrafts, tomorrow." I headed for the cabin.

"Where have you been?" the storekeeper asked.

"Why?"

"Your girls have been down in their pajamas wanting to know where their counselor is. It's after ten."

Sixteen teenage girls were excitedly chattering—lights on. "Where were you?"

"I have a beautiful secret to share with you, if you'll go right to bed and right to sleep."

They did, but I didn't! That was a miracle.

All night long I laid on my cot grinning. What will people think? Here I've warned my young people to be very sure they know their mate before the wedding, for it should be for life.

Here I was engaged to a man the fourth time I'd even seen him.

I thought of Audrey. She'll think I went off my rocker because she gave me that silly bouquet. She did.

Next morning, all the girls went dashing off for flag raising and devotions. I was the last to leave. I heard a sound in the bushes.

"How soon can we get married? I've waited a long time for you. Now I can hardly wait."

"It can't be for a couple of months, at least. I have to give my mission a month's notice and, since you are the presiding elder of your church, we will have to have a church wedding. I don't have a thing that I can't put in a suitcase. It would take a month to prepare."

"Make it as soon as you can."

I was to give my bird program that morning, so he took Mother in the back door and I went in the front. After I finished, Kieth Benson, the director, informed, "We're all going on a scavenger hunt and a wiener roast. We'll get back just in time for the evening meeting."

"Does that mean there'll be no handicrafts?" hopefully.

He turned, "How many of you kids would rather go to handicrafts than with us?" About twenty-five hands went up. I sighed.

"Ah, you kids don't want to go to handicrafts this afternoon. You know your counselor was out kind of late last night and I think she needs a little vacation," he said with a mischievous grin. They roared with laughter.

Bissell assigned someone to care for Mother. We jumped in his car and sped down the mountain. "What kind of ring do you want, honey? One of those big blazers a migrant would knock you over the head to get off your finger?"

"Oh no! That's not my style. I'd like the ring I saw in my thoughts last night. It had three perfect little diamonds set low in a gold band and a plain gold wedding band to match. I could use it as an object lesson: the three diamonds would represent the trinity; the gold, deity; and the engagement ring, the time we accepted His love and were separated unto Him until the marriage of the Lamb in Heaven."

"That's a wonderful idea, but where could we find such a ring?"

"There's a Christian jeweler in Dinuba who has been very kind to us."

"He's a friend of mine and is on the Hume Lake board. We'll go there."

"Well, of all the couples who come through this door, I don't know of anyone I'd rather see coming in arm-in-arm."

He covered the counters with glittering sets. One large diamond skirted with two or four on each side was the present style. Then he remembered, "I have a ring in the safe with three of equal size." He put it on my finger.

"That's it," I marveled. "That's the one I saw! It fits perfectly!"

He slipped on the gold band.

"They match perfectly!"

I glanced at the price tag, "Oh, I hope I haven't chosen one he isn't able to pay for. I know he makes lots of money, but he gives it all away. I hope I haven't caused him embarrassment."

He didn't look at the price. "If that's the ring she wants, that's the ring she's gonna have."

"We'll be leaving in a couple of days, and I'd like to see the home on the ranch," I suggested.

He had offered me a choice of either of the nice new homes he had built for rental or the old one he had built for his mother, who had gone to heaven twenty years ago. I told him I'd rather have a shack in the country than a palace in town. He was pleased.

"If I'd known you wanted to see it, I'd have gotten it all cleaned up," he apologized.

"That's all right." I saw the cobwebs, the unused rooms, the path from the back door to the bed. He was so lonely, he spent little time at home.

"It just makes me love you all the more because I know you need me. I can dream while I'm away of how I can make it into a real home again."

We went by to see the pastor and arrange for our wedding. Bissell was instrumental in the designing and building of a beautiful new church. Teasingly, they had said he was building it for his wedding. "I am going to have my wedding in it," Bissell insisted jubilantly. "so you better get to work and finish it in time."

"I want you to meet an older couple who recently were married." Bissell took me to a small farm in the edge of town. "They were in love for many years, but her parents refused. Finally, they went ahead and now her parents claim him as their favorite son-in-law."

"Oh, I know you," Ethel exclaimed. "You spoke for the Christian Business and Professional Women's Club in Spokane, Washington. I'd like to make your wedding gown, if you'd furnish the materials." Bissell furnished that.

When we returned to Hume, the secretary wanted to see my hand. I played innocent. Bissell had a whole stack of white shirts his foreman's wife had left for him, but we forgot to take them so I was washing and ironing the only one with him. "Why are you ironing a man's shirt?" they prodded. It's hard to keep secrets in a place like that.

Friday, at the banquet, Keith held up an envelope, "To Keith and the Kids," he read. On Hume stationery, I had drawn hearts on two sheets. The first said: "God made this…" Then, I taped a wooden match. The second said: "Bissell Garrett and Juanita McComb." We were in an avalanche of kids, leaders, conference folks and cabin owners.

Volunteers took care of my mother and the three boys so that we could have an evening in Mrs. Shearer's home. She left us alone. Nothing seemed strange—it was as if we had always belonged to each other and to the plans He had for our future

CHAPTER 19

Always Bring Children

Mother, the three boys and I headed for Rescue with a box of the largest peaches I ever saw; Bissell had brought them. After returning the boys with an experience in Christian living and fellowship, we went on to Cool.

A grandma had brought her grandchildren to our VBS in Rescue. She also came into a new relationship as well. It was her burden for her daughters and family that opened the door to Cool. Since no one wanted to open their homes to us, Grandma let us use an old tavern she had purchased; it had been their family farm. She hated the thought of it being desecrated by a liquor store.

I scrubbed and cleaned, but it still stunk. We put benches together to sleep on, using things from my little trailer. We made do, all right.

For the VBS, the mothers brought their children and, while I tried to teach, they sat in the back in constant chatter. They didn't invite us to eat lunch with them, so we drove back to share a can of soup and return to teach them handicrafts.

Near the end of our two weeks, Grandma came to visit her daughter. I don't know what she said, but the next day we were invited to a good picnic dinner and they gave me my first shower. Friends from Sacramento came to carry on the Sunday services and God sent a hunger for God; a church was born.

Our mission conference came next at Cannon Beach, Oregon—one of my most loved beaches and conference grounds. Precious memories still delight my thoughts of fellowship enjoyed.

On their way from HQ in Kansas City, Mrs. Baugh and Miss Clark discussed problems, "Public enemy number one is man. Just as soon as we get a team of fine missionaries serving the Lord, up comes an eligible bachelor and captures them." They named Verle, Dorothy, Audrey and others. "But there's one who won't desert us—that's Juanita McComb. She's just married to the Lord."

They pulled up in front of the lodge. A girl ran to greet them, "Mrs. Baugh, guess what! Juanita McComb is getting married!"

"Oh no!"

Letters came every other day. Friends claimed they could tell by the glow on my face. Clubs arranged for me to speak all the way to LA; Each one had a shower. At the big Church of the Open Door, a friend ran across the room when I arrived, "Juanita! I heard you were getting married. I heard about it in Alaska."

Back in Fresno, Mrs. Shearer arranged for Mother's care so we could prepare for the church wedding. In spite of harvest time, the friends went into high gear to get the stained glass windows in, the auditorium cleaned and filled with folding chairs. I set up my bird-picture scenery with a central arbor, and they covered the floor with sheets and banks of flowers. Over four hundred came. Lorna was my bridesmaid and her little Ann, the ring bearer. Don French was the best man.

At the reception, the old church was so full of gifts it looked like a department store.

No one deserves to receive so much, I thought.

As soon as I had left after our engagement, Bissell hired workmen to remodel the home so we would have room for young people's meeting. He added ten feet on the front and twelve feet on the side, so we had a big room for games and devotional times. We worked hard to get it ready to move into as soon as we were married, but it was still being plastered. Friends had come so far, we couldn't run off. By the time we did get away, we were too tired to go to Hume.

"Let's just go to bed in the army tent and get away before the workmen come," I advised. It was midmorning when we awoke. We got so busy with the men, it was evening and we were again tired out.

"There's no place to stop here, and I don't want to miss out on a honeymoon."

Bissell took the wheel. He went off the road a time or two as sleep overcame him, so I did the driving. At the cabin, we slept most of the time.

The rainy season was due, so we worked long hours to get out of the open-top army tent. One day too late—rain soaked his photo albums and I ironed them with twenty-three white shirts the next few days.

Ethel and Alf stored our gifts until we were ready; the truckload of gifts filled the big room. If I had spent months choosing color harmonies and outfitting each room and the cabin, I couldn't have done such a good job. The Lord had planned all the details to exceeding perfection, above all I could ask or think!

We gave all to the Lord, but He gave more than we could ever use—I'm still giving away wedding presents. Mother was with my older sister and family while we got settled. We set up the bed she and her sisters and brothers were born in. Her room was filled with her most treasured antiques from her beautiful girlhood home. Her paintings were hung. Bissell was as devoted to her as he had been to his own mother.

The church came for a house-warming before we had finished. We found the toilet on top of the roof and the canned foods were all de-labeled. I learned to open a can first and plan a meal around its contents.

One day, I was folding the egg whites into an angel food cake when Bissell called me to drive tractor for him. When I returned, I tried to finish mixing it. When it came out of the oven, we named it Lucifer—it was a fallen angel.

The beautiful church in which we were married became a part of the National and then the World Council of Churches and began to teach a social gospel. The pastor asked us not to talk about sin or false doctrines lest we hurt someone's feelings.

"If I can't teach my adult class the truth right out of the Book, I'm through," Bissell told me. He had to go to the hospital for a cataract operation. "This is as good a time as any to make a change. You go to the little Baptist church in Caruthers and see how you like it."

The Barrams were pastoring there at the time; he was tops. That first Sunday, the teacher for the high school class was absent, so I filled in. The pastor's two teenage sons announced to their parents, "We want her for our teacher."

"We don't proselyte. Pray about it."

For the next six years, I taught that class, coming eighty-five miles back from Hume each weekend for the four summer months. They met in our home for fun and fellowship on Thursdays and at the church for Sunday school. It grew from a few to an average of fifty, until our fine pastor went on to a larger church and we got a couple of men who tried to make the young people leave us and submit to their authority. They wouldn't respond; there wasn't the love and challenge to go all out for the Lord. The Lord used a jealous pastor to scatter our young people and make us willing to go to Ireland.

CHAPTER 20

Adapting By Christ

"A FAITHFUL MAN SHALL ABOUND WITH BLESSINGS"
—PROV. 28:20

Count on it: When He takes a precious ministry away from you, He has something far better beyond your horizon awaiting you—the next step in your faith walk. Our sight is limited to visible experience, but the mighty, omniscient God sees far beyond our narrow vision. When my husband and I were obedient to His leading, the adventures of the next chapter were beyond storybook tales.

At sixty-five, Bissell began the process of retirement by selling his trucks. Then, the Lord told him to sell his ranches. "The value of the property is worth more than you can realize in profit in your lifetime."

I had told him when we were married that I wanted him to do his giving while he was living, so he would know where it was going. "I don't know anything about raising raisins. If you precede me, knowing nothing about selling property, I might not get its true value. God entrusted it to you. I lived by faith before I married you, and I can live by faith after you're gone. I don't want that responsibility."

As Bissell prayed, God said to sell. "If you are speaking to me, Lord, you send the buyer. I won't list it with a realtor."

Soon, I was in the yard when a neighbor walked over from the next farm. "Are you willing to sell that ranch on Mt. View?"

"You'll have to talk to my husband. He'll be back this evening."

"It isn't good to raise a family on rented ground," he told Bissell. "That twenty acres has a good enough house and just what I want."

"The water level has gone down, so I've irrigated from the well across the road. You'd have to go deeper for your water supply."

"I have been saving for a long time, so I'd have enough for that too." The deal was closed.

Months later, we were in the little town of Caruthers getting electrical supplies. As we stepped out, a realtor stopped him. "Bissell, are you willing to sell that property on Mt. View? The man who has the adjoining ranch is very anxious to expand. He'll pay a good price."

Shortly, the transaction was completed.

"By the way, would you, by any chance, be willing to sell your home place?"

"I don't want to give Uncle Sam so much tax."

"The family who wants it, goes to your church. They have practically no down payment, but would pay interest over a long period."

"That sounds like a good deal." The Fresno Rescue Mission had started a ranch in the foothills to take men and boys who had professed their faith to go for rehabilitation. They wanted us to help with it. "Their payments could be our support," he reasoned.

We began packing. It was hard to give up the only home I'd ever had. There were seven years of precious memories. "Your will is my will, Lord. This world is not my home. I'm just a passing through. My treasures are laid up somewhere beyond the blue." I sang as I packed my beautiful wedding gifts in boxes, many of which I wouldn't see again for ten years or more.

I painted a mural for the Fresno Rescue Mission. (25 years later, I visited that mission. The present director was out of my youth group.) "There have been more messages given using that picture as an illustration than anything else," he explained. I had painted the city of Destruction with a cross as a bridge to the city of God. The narrow gate led to the High Way, but the broad way went down to the great gulf that led to the fires of judgment.

I had completed a 4' x 8' picture for the mission in San Jose that was started by a couple who were like our own family. Lester Myers was gloriously saved in the Fresno Rescue Mission one Christmas. We were used of God to encourage them as they started the San Jose Rescue Mission.

🐿 🐿 🐿

As we pulled in, the phone announced to tired ears, "There's a special meeting at church tonight. A preacher from Portugal is speaking through an interpreter."

"I don't think we'll go, I'm too tired. I don't think a message through an interpreter would be very interesting anyway." He hung up. He thought a while. "Maybe we ought to go to encourage them. There may not be many who turn out."

Dr. Ben Pierson, a missionary who had lived through the "blood bath" in Colombia when so many Christians were killed and churches blown up, was the interpreter for Antonio Martines. Telling the story of his conversion, persecution and the birth of the Baptist churches in Portugal was an unforgettable story of God's grace and power.

Tony told of the secret seminary and academy to train leaders and the desperate need for literature. Bissell was all ears. As people left, he approached them with, "If you need any books from the Fresno Bible House, I'll pay up to $100." That night he was sharing a burden for those behind the purple curtain who had little chance to hear the gospel.

Next morning, I reasoned, "Bissell, we haven't heard from the mission about going to their ranch, and we have to move out very soon. You better go in and find out why."

All of the leaders at the mission had gone to a conference, so he went on to the Bible House. There was Tony hugging an armful of books. "I've always wanted these and never could afford them."

"If it means that much to you, go in and get all you want."

They went to the prayer room. The Spirit blended their hearts in love. Most of the night he talked about the needs in Portugal. Early next morning, the phone carried Dr. Ben's voice, "Tony wants to come and see you. He says God gave him a sermon for you. Are you willing to listen?"

As soon as the car could come the sixteen miles, they sat in our living room. "When I came to this country, my main burden was for a hospital where anyone could go safely. Each time I spoke, the Lord led me to share the need for literature. I'm to return soon and I still haven't told of the need for a hospital. Last night, the Lord said I should tell you."

He explained about the powerful, Roman-Catholic-controlled government. If a Protestant had to go to a hospital, he had to recant his faith and kiss the feet of the Virgin in order to be admitted. "Even then," he pleaded, "they usually come out feet first." He dreamed of a hospital where anyone could go safely and wouldn't be cheated financially, as well.

"How much would it cost?

"Seventy-five thousand."

"I don't have that much."

"God didn't say how much He wants you to give. Whatever it is, that will assure us that God will raise the rest through others."

Before we returned from Ireland, we visited that hospital. Bissell wept for joy as he realized that, in the three years it had been open, three thousand patients had used the operating table. The people revered Antonio Martines because he made it possible.

"But that isn't all God told me," Tony continued. "He wants you, too."

"What could I do? I don't know the language."

"You could be the director of the hospital."

"Oh no," I butted in, "he doesn't know the first thing about hospitals."

"Would you mind taking care of the garden and grounds?"

"That would be right down my alley."

"And He wants you, too," he turned to me. "We need teachers for the girls."

"But I don't know Portuguese."

"We teach in English because we can't get books in our language."

He explained that, as the head of the Baptist churches, they would send an official invitation. They went on their way with boxes of our encyclopedias and all they could use from our large library.

🐦 🐦 🐦

Returning from the Rescue Mission conference, they informed us that they were not able to finance the ranch and that's why they didn't know sooner. They didn't want us to move in and then have to give it up.

After much prayer and the invitation came, we began packing for overseas. We sent out our first prayer letter. The one to the seminary had been opened before it reached the missionaries. We got an SOS from a missionary just returning on furlough. We met him in San Jose.

"I hope this won't disappoint you," he was almost in tears. "We need you, but if you come according to the plan in your letter, the authorities will be laying for you. It would endanger our work, too. You could come in on a tourist visa for a couple of months, but would have to leave; it's illegal to come in as missionaries. When they censored your letter, they figured you would bring the gospel."

"Don't worry about us being disappointed," I comforted him. "God has led us this far for a reason. If it isn't to Portugal, I wouldn't want to go there."

CHAPTER 21

Always Beware Counterfeits

ON TO IRELAND

We were helping our dear friends Lester and Pauline Meyers with the mission in San Jose, at the time. I was in the Meyer's home explaining the turn of events, "There's a mission that has similar problems in the south of Ireland. Their HQ is right here. It's a small one, but good," she said. She gave me the material. After reading about their ministries, I phoned.

"What we need are teachers," the missionary just back for furlough explained.

"I'm a teacher."

"Can we come right over?"

"No, Bissell is at the mission until nine o'clock, and we won't discuss anything without being together on it." It was finally agreed they could come at eight o'clock and hear of my training and experience and, if they felt I would fill the need in the Irish Bible Institute, they could stay and talk to Bissell.

"We've never had anyone as old as you are, but I'll present your qualifications to Mr. Steel. If he's interested, he'll make an appointment.

As we sat in his office the next day, we were impressed by that saintly man who had lived through the horrors of German and Russian prisons through the war and was moved with compassion for the host of orphaned children. He swore that if he lived through the ordeal, he would start homes to nurture all he could of destitute children. God restored his health enough to start homes in several countries.

We told him of selling our property and using the money for the Lord's work.

"If you have any money for the Lord's work, I don't want you to give it to our mission. Where money is involved, it's too hard to know the mind of the Holy Spirit."

That assured us of his genuine love.

"If you are accepted by the board, it would be advisable to save enough to be self-supporting. It's very hard for older folks to raise support."

The next five weeks, we were living at the mission and our cabin in Hume. We had jumped so fast at the call to Portugal, we felt we wanted to be very sure of the next step.

"A ship can't be guided until it starts moving," I told Bissell one morning. "If the Lord doesn't want us to go, there are all those doors He can close. There's our age, doctrinal differences or health the board would have to pass on."

Bissell sat down immediately and filled out the application. I spent hours filling mine out. If I was to teach in the Bible Institute, I wanted them to know for sure what I believed and would teach. It was a thorough examination and I gave proof texts of every doctrine.

Almost the next mail welcomed us to HQ for orientation. A whirl of responsibilities followed. I had done four thousand dollars worth of business in my handicrafts shop at Hume Lake, besides keeping young helpers in our cabin and shop. There was the packing to be done. We hauled thirty-four large trunks and boxes to be shipped by sea.

One of the older ladies at church wanted to take care of Mother. We made arrangements for our mission to take her to the care home they ran, if Auntie Ryan couldn't handle her.

We got her moved in with all her own things surrounding her. When I had to say good-bye she wanted to know where I was going.

"I'm going to work," I smiled, kissed and hugged her.

"Do a good job," she replied.

Out of sight, I sobbed. I knew I'd not see her again this side of heaven.

We couldn't reach Ireland before the first of October. We drove almost non-stop to Lincoln. There, my sister had arranged a farewell gathering of relatives and close friends. Our former pastor and wife came. He had been the preacher at the church I joined after I accepted the Lord. Now he was the head of the seminary in Lincoln.

The time Audrey and I took Mother to Lincoln, she wanted to attend that church and see old friends. The big church was crowded.

The topic of his message was "Define Your Terms." He told jokes of funny results where people said one thing, but meant another.

"Now we should investigate the benefits of Communism," he began. "The first Christians were Communists—they had everything in common." That was the only statement that had anything to do with the Word of God. There were some things in Russian Communism he didn't agree with, but American Communism is quite a different thing.

The well-dressed throng filed out, telling him how good it was to see him and hear his delightful message. I avoided him and boiled inside.

Here he was smiling his way into the party. I went to my niece, "Pray for me Marie as I give the message, I may never get back and many of these dear ones are unsaved. I'm going to tell it like it is. It's my only chance to give them the gospel.

After sharing my testimony of the new life I received—when I put my trust in the Savior who died in my place to pay for my sins and rose for my justification—I shared, in as condensed a form as possible, of how He led me and then us to go to Ireland.

Then, as gently as I could, I tried to show how religion without a surrender to the Lord Jesus Christ was futile.

"When I was in high school, we went to church at least five times a week. We supported it, and I tried to serve my Savior with my whole heart; but I saw much hypocrisy and received very little Bible teaching. I feel I was cheated. I struggled along for years striving to please God, ignorant of the grace and power of the Holy Spirit to apply God's Word to my daily walk."

The pastor glared at me. Demonic lights pierced through his eyes. He got up and walked out. I never saw him again. I hope he repented of his sins and has turned from the apostasy of the counterfeit churches who are headed by Satan. If he and those who follow the social gospel do not obey the Way, the Truth and the Life, their destiny will be with the condemnation of their master.

Reaching our friends in New York, we turned our station wagon over as a gift to Mr. Steel to use for deputation on the way back.

Durand Hummel took us to our ship, the North American, and we were on board when news came that a strike was called. It might be days before sailing. No effort was made to help us on our way, so Durand rushed over to the German Lines. The Hanseatic was about to leave. If we rushed we could transfer.

We ran up the gangplank. "Don't worry, it will all be on board some place," they shouted, tossing our luggage over the widening gap as the big liner eased away from the dock. It took all week to locate all sixteen pieces, but it was with us. Our stateroom was much nicer. The cabin boy was a fine Christian and, every spare moment he could be with us, we enjoyed the fellowship. This was to be his last trip. He could continue his training for the Lord.

I was able to have children's meetings. Most of the daylight hours, Bissell was on the top deck worshipping the God who made it all. "To think, God's love and grace is greater than this ocean," he marveled.

A small ship came out to meet the huge liner as we reached Ireland. With much fanfare, we were transferred and went through customs at Cove.

"You can't tell me you aren't Irish, with those red lips and rosy cheeks," the officer surmised.

"I'm Scotch-Irish," I answered. "My name was 'McComb' before I got married. Then I lost my 'comb,'" I joked. We laughed and he passed us on without opening a thing. As the Irish green countryside flashed by, I knelt at the train window and fell in love with Ireland.

We were met in Dublin and taken the fifty miles to Drewstown House. We were shown to our third-floor apartment. The room had a table, a built-in bench and wooden platform for our bed. How thankful we brought a foam pad to cover the hard board. A sink, little kitchenette and fireplace gave me hopes of making it a lovely place.

Looking out of the round end of the room the view was breathtaking: Swans glided on the lake, a stone bridge, great trees and rushes made a masterpiece of scenery.

As we sat at our first meal they sang, "There's a welcome here…a Christian welcome here." But, as I glanced at some faces, there was anger reflected. Some were not smiling. As I started to unpack, Bissell took a tour of the building. Out of sight, he heard two women.

"I was supposed to start that welcome song!"

"No, I wanted to. That is my job."

They quarreled.

"If I was not absolutely sure God sent us to this place, we'd put our hats on and leave this very day." Bissell hated fights as much as I did.

I started teaching my subjects, but, there again was a battle going on: Half the students accepted the fundamentals; the others sided with the principal. They claimed they were not allowed to read a Schofield Bible or any of the evangelical writings. They had all they could do to keep up with his assignments.

"What is it you are teaching?" I confronted the principal. "Didn't you sign the same doctrinal questionnaire I did?"

"Yes, that was what Mr. Steel wanted. I had a professor once who believed that pre-millennial stuff. I wanted to come so I figured I could teach it to please him, but when I got over here I found some others who didn't believe it either, so I'm teaching it to suit myself."

"Well I can't make any headway in my classes because of their arguing. What is it you teach?"

He handed me a book and I read it. It reminded me of Swiss cheese—it was full of holes. It was like Limburger cheese—it stunk.

I was to be the speaker for every other assembly. The students wanted more as they came to know and love me. Often, he would jump up and rudely cut me off.

Some other missionaries joined us in hours of prayer for that couple. The principal and his wife often would come to us with their problems and we prayed with them, hoping they would see the light. They had asked us to also take over the girls, but I said Mr. Steel emphatically insisted I was not there as a house mother to the girls of the home; I was the Bible Institute teacher only.

🦜 🦜 🦜

I went to Dublin to get needed furniture for our apartment. A Rescue Mission for women had just closed and I bought a trailer-load of chairs and a recliner. When the load of chairs was backed up to the steps, the two women rushed out and grabbed as fast as they could. Not one was left for us. The recliner chair I kept. There was a backless chair in the library. I asked if I could have it. I repaired another so we could sit at the table.

The furnace was fed by a chain drive that fed sawdust into the firebox to heat that big building. It was Bissell's job to keep it going. The van they hauled the sawdust in from the mill was a wreck. They were praying for a new one. They had seven hundred dollars saved, but vans were thousands. We saw no way to keep them warm without one, so we paid the rest and we all rejoiced in the shiny new van to take us to church and town.

Soon, the principal forbade the students to go to church, "If they are to master all my assignments, they need that time to study."

I was one of the speakers for the Child Evangelism Conference in Belfast during the Christmas holidays, so I joined the students for the short trip to the train line.

How much is my share of the gas?" I asked as we started.

"A pound." The principal held out his hand.

"He shouldn't have charged you a pound for that little way. We only paid a shilling."

"Maybe he needed money for gas. It's OK."

They had complained so loudly that they had no money to visit their son in Liverpool that I gave up all my allowance so they could go. When they returned, they were completely outfitted with nice new clothes and shoes. The girls came to us. "How come they claim they don't have money to buy a postage stamp, but they come back like the rich?"

"Maybe someone gave them a Christmas gift."

In Belfast, I stayed with a missionary who was instrumental in sending one of our students. Knowing something was not right at the Bible school, she kept prodding me. Brenda had shared her thoughts, but I tried to keep my burdens before the Lord. Finally, I burst into sobs.

"When you return, I'm going with you," she declared. She was akin to a detective. She discovered he had asked a rank liberal to teach the Bible school the next year. When she confronted him, he denied it. But, with the facts in hand, she hounded him till he confessed.

"But the prospectus hasn't gone to the printers yet," was his excuse for lying.

That evening, the principal stood up and confessed to lying. To all present, his confession seemed so genuine he was forgiven. It looked like a real spirit of revival and we all rejoiced. Later, though, he and his wife were laughing about the clever way he put it across. There was no sense of guilt as he told me, "That's what they wanted."

Later, the mission board, Mr. Pazeley and Mrs. Sharples, who had sent students, came to personally examine him. The principal went right down the list of the doctrines we had signed before ending with, "This is what I teach."

They looked at one another, then to him, "That is what we believe and want taught." After they left, he and his wife were having a big laugh. Again, they had put it across. The rest of the year, the students were taught the modernist doctrines. It was hard to teach the students the truth without condemning the errors he was forcing on them. We prayed the Holy Spirit would give them discernment. Looking back, He did.

One of the women came in tears and asked my forgiveness for her jealousy of me—I had it all together. I was happy and she wasn't. We hugged and praised God.

We had a Christmas program early. I brought lots of costumes along for the wise men and shepherds. They looked so cute with the beards and pretty robes. The people came for miles around to see the pageant they put on annually.

I built bookshelves in our apartment and the library to accommodate the big trunk full of Christian books from our home. The sixteen school-age children spent as much time up in our apartment as possible. The children's books and toys were appreciated.

Before going to Ireland, I gathered many stuffed animals and dolls, removed the stuffing, washed them and used them as packing for dishes, etc. When I restuffed them, they were the nicest toys they had ever seen.

We became fond of all the children as well as the students. Neil was a quiet, thoughtful little boy of 6. He didn't fit in with the other outgoing rambunctious kids. One day he came with a dust cloth trying to be my helper. "Can I be your little boy?" he showed how good a duster he was. How we longed to claim him as our son, but were not allowed to.

CHAPTER 22

Adopting Beloved Children
AVOCA MANOR BABY HOME

For Easter holiday, we went the hundred miles to Avoca Manor where the preschool children were. They were so adorable, we hated to leave. We had no idea that, in a couple of months, we would become their foster parents and love them as much as if we had given birth to them.

As the school year closed, our mission founder, Mr. Steel, was not expected to live; the field directors were called back to headquarters. Bob Minter was in charge of Austria and Ireland; his wife May ran the baby home.

We were asked to take over, suddenly. Only the Lord could transform a sixty-eight-year-old farmer and his fifty-one-year-old wife into foster parents in the few days of indoctrination into the mysteries of: Irish currency, driving on the left side of the road, 220-volt electricity that came in surges or failed, of shopping wholesale in the crooked streets of Dublin, and the daily care of sixteen precious souls—eight in diapers, the rest were preschoolers.

Although Brian was fourteen, he was unable to even sign his name. James was like a frightened wild animal when he came. He was also a slow learner, but both boys had the most tender hearts, they never forgot a kindness.

Wee Jimmie was in the hospital when we came. He was a frail pre-mature baby and nearly died when he got whooping cough, just before we took over. May had prayed for him as she raced him to the hospital—God answered. When we went to pick him up, he took one look at Uncle Bissell and went right into his arms and heart. They were inseparable the remainder of our time in Ireland. He would share half of Uncle Bissell with the others.

These were unadoptable as long as a parent was living. If the parent ever wanted to take their child we had to give them up. We trusted the Lord to see them mature as we ministered to their body, soul and spirit. We felt that if they were loved, taught the Word and could see the fruit of the Spirit in our daily walk, they would always remember the times we feasted together at our Master's table and would return to the Heavenly Father.

Avoca Manor was a beautiful mansion overlooking the famed Vale of Avoca in Irish songs. The switchback drive from the highway was lined by ferns, giant trees and flowers of every hue. The home had been designed and built by an artist. While we were there, his son came from America to visit his childhood home. "My father should have been an architect instead of a rector." He smiled as he admired the exquisite carvings over the fireplaces and stained-glass windows he had done.

We had been told of the conversion of the Densmores. God had led them to sell out and buy another fine, old mansion to rescue orphan boys. The night after they moved in, masked men ordered, "If you want to get out with your life, get out now!" Mr. Densmore was allowed to take the clock his employees had given as a farewell love gift. All the rest went up in smoke as they poured gasoline over the floors. They had successfully removed the "Protestant heretics" they thought.

Brokenhearted, they looked to the Lord, "Why, God? We put everything we have into making a home for these boys."

"Trust me. I will meet all your needs my way."

Sympathetic friends sent gifts. Avoca Manor was for sale with sealed bids. They put all there was in an envelope and turned it in. By an act of God, that home became His orphanage. As they moved in, two armed guards came. "We are here to prevent the Legion of Mary from burning this home, too."

"We know God has given us this place, so we trust Him to protect it," they assured them.

"We have our orders." For the next two years, they were under police protection twenty-four hours a day. The love for the Densmores, their boys and the God who directed them, made their remaining years a shining testimony to the transforming power of the Lord.

"Mr. Densmore used to be quite a rounder," one old-timer told me, "but something happened and he changed."

Granny Densmore was still in the home when we came. We felt the Spirit of God radiating from her work-worn old body. If I remember right, thirty-six boys were rescued, loved, taught and sent on to live fruitful lives with a couple of exceptions. When Mr. Densmore was dying, he wanted World Mission to Children to inherit the home and start rescuing Protestant babies who were without protection.

Admiring the magnificent furniture in the drawing room and parlor, Granny shared how God had given abundantly. At the sale, they saw mahogany furnishings that just seemed to belong to its setting and wished the Lord had given them more so they could bid. The sale ended. The lady came with the long list of her purchases and gave it to them.

She told how the Church of Ireland rector wanted to build his dream house. He got the land donated by a local farmer for a rectory. Then he went to America, posed as a Catholic priest and got enough donations to build an orphanage.

The Catholic builders felt he was a jolly good fellow and liked the pay. The dream house became a palatial home for his family, but the orphans never came. The farmer tried to get him defrocked, but he was able to evade the law till God's time to turn it over to the Densmores for an orphanage.

How we all loved Granny—that dear old saint! But then she had a stroke; it was our joy to care for her.

Each night, after devotions with my boys, each one prayed his own prayer as I knelt by his bed. I loved each of them intimately as I prayed for him.

"What made Granny all crippled up like that?" James asked.

"She just got all worn out working for her boys."

"You work hard for us boys. Will you get that way when you get old?"

"Well, maybe I will."

"Who'll mind you when you get like that?"

"Oh, I don't know. Maybe one of my boys."

"I know which one."

"Which one?"

"Me," proudly. My heart turned a flip. I knew he couldn't, but his love was genuine. Later, he said when he grew up he was going to be a farmer, drive a tractor, and take care of Uncle Bissell and Aunt Birdie. Both boys who were unable to learn in school had the super gift of loving appreciation and deep sympathy for anyone or thing that was hurting.

Babies grow unbelievably fast. It was time to separate boys and girls. The eight boys were my chief responsibility. We taught them to be our little helpers. Uncle Bissell got all the breakfasts, did the dishes and spent the rest of the day in the big play room or the yard, weather permitting. All the little ones swarmed over him like bees over honey. He loved them; they adored him.

Blind Winston went on to Bible school in France. Robin called me twenty years later from Canada when he learned my new name and address.

"I'm here because of the encouragement you gave." He explained how the Lord had led and blessed him in a ministry and a master's degree. He ended the long phone call, "Now my one great desire before the rapture is to see your face again."

When two of my Irish boys graduated from Prairie Bible Institute, Paul went on with us across Canada to Hamilton, Ontario, to spend a week with him and his family. Robin called again the other day. God is still blessing.

Now Paul Montgomery earned another degree at La Tourneau U - cum laude. God has given him a wonderful wife and four precious children. Phil pastors a church in Ireland. Tony graduated from Mont. Bl and is very successful. His wife is the daughter of missionaries in Alaska. They have two brilliant sons.

CHAPTER 23

Appreciating Bissell's Christianity

GOING HOME TO JESUS

Brethren, we do not want you to be ignorant about those who have fallen asleep, or to grieve like the rest of men, who have no hope. We believe that Jesus died and rose again and so we believe that God will bring with Jesus those who have fallen asleep in Him. (1 Thessalonians 4:13–14)

Beloved in the Lord, this chapter started near Carter, South Dakota, in September 1965. At long last, a wee lull has come in the pressures of responsibilities that have filled each day since that morning when our precious Lord ushered my beloved into His glorious presence.

Precious are the memories of the events leading up to Uncle Bissell's "coronation." Join in praise and adoration for the grace of God in our behalf; He has met every need.

Some of you know of the two and a half years of our faith walk after we returned from our five years in Ireland. Only God knew of Bissell's desire to experience the thrill of total dependence on God to meet needs in answer to prayer. In his ministry of giving, he gave thousands yearly—keeping only for necessities—but he knew the hard work it took on his part. Now that we were not permitted to carry on the loving care of the foster family in Ireland, the support from the sale of our property, that had kept the mission from losing both homes, would no longer be misused by nationals. They felt, because we gave so much, that we were fabulously wealthy, so they bled us for all they could get. They didn't realize that as payments came in we gave it all, for we saw the needs and met them. We knew of dishonest practices, but they wouldn't let us see the bookkeeping to prove their misappropriation of funds.

While I was on a trip through Europe as a guest of my niece and husband, Bissell rested in our apartment in Drewstown and decided to save just enough to buy our new VW van. He also saved enough to see the Old Mill in Austria, the hospital in Portugal that his giving had made possible, and to get us back to Florida. Then, he wanted to see if God would meet our needs as He had for me before we were married. The rest he gave to another ministry.

God honored his desire. Disembarking in Jacksonville, Florida, we had sixteen dollars to cross the U.S. We told no one of any needs for the next two and a half years—a remarkable witness of the unique ways God answered our prayers is a story in itself.

One year we were house parents for the summer, and I taught through the school year at the mission school. Then, we met an SOS call from Audrey, my former missionary teammate. They had been hospitalized from a car wreck.

"What do you need?" we queried.

"Food."

We rented our little home to make the payments and loaded our van with the canned foods given by our church. All summer we helped with American Sunday schools, VBS and camps for ranchers and Indians.

A new Nike site was offered as an academy for needy boys. We were begged to help staff this million-dollar plant. Reactivating it was hard after five years of vacancy. Month after month, the head of welfare added more requirements before she would give a license. We could have three hundred boys supported by welfare. The last month, she proved she had no intention of licensing as long as we taught the Bible. Those three boys we had were privately supported.

A terrible blizzard caused great loss. Jerry battled the blizzard to come to our building to make sure we were all right. With no heat, light or water we kept moving—filling cracks.

"Why are you doing all this?" he wondered. "You aren't getting paid for it."

"Oh no," we assured him, "we're putting everything we have into making this a good home and school for you boys."

"Well, I want you to know this is the first time in all my life that anyone did anything for me without getting paid for it." He shared the trauma of a wretched childhood. He learned through our love that he had a Heavenly Father who loved him all the time and a Savior who died for him.

The nine months before we were forced to close, were fruitful. The three boys finished eighth grade and many of the neglected children of the military housing across the fence spent all their spare time with us while their moms played cards and drank.

A rancher offered me a teaching position in a country school with only four children. A little home across from the rancher's home and a good salary sounded like a good place for Bissell to rest and help the rancher as he was able. I signed the contract with the understanding that I could share Bible answers for any spiritual questions. A Christian rancher loaned us his big truck to take all our possessions to be stored through the summer in the teacherage, and we returned with a load of steers for a Christian college. Back we went with our van load.

The former teacher and her husband were allowed to leave their things until they finished building a home in Winner. We had to empty one bedroom in order to stack our things there.

The family who rented our little home in Oregon wanted to buy it, so we visited relatives and loved ones en route. We reached the most treasured spot on earth in time for a Hume Lake board meeting. Bissell and five other dedicated men had prayed for, sacrificed and worked to make a camp for underprivileged children. Through a chain of miracles, it had grown to reach many thousands of people of all ages. After seven years of absence, he was thrilled to be with many of his dearest friends. They took him to show him all the new developments.

"This is the vestibule to heaven." He had a delightful week. Home owners were there, too, and we were lavished with love.

We stopped to visit a dear family who had come to know the Lord while Audrey and I were missionaries. Paul had lost almost everything as an alcoholic and hoped for victory in a new environment and the encouragement of his brother who was newly saved. They arrived the last day of our fortnight of special meetings. The story of their conversion was described previously. To be near us, they built a cabin at Hume Lake higher than ours; but before it was finished, we went to Ireland and sold ours. Upon our return from Ireland we visited them. Giving us the keys and loading our van with food, they said their cabin was ours anytime. So that is where we stayed that week. On the way up the mountain, we stopped for gas and a few store needs.

"Do you want me to check the oil?" the attendant asked.

"You needn't bother," Bissell answered. "We never use any between changes."

Ten miles from our destination, I heard a knock, checked the oil and found it nearly gone. I added oil and sluggishly climbed on up nearly to the cabin when the motor stopped. Friends were in back of us, and we emptied the van and his old pal Don French took it to the garage.

"You needn't rush to check it over. We'll be here all week." Bissell didn't want to add to the Lord's day and board meeting fellowship. We took inventory. We had fifty-seven dollars to our name.

"That won't buy a new motor, but maybe it isn't as bad as we think it is," I assured him.

"It's all my fault. I should have had that man check the oil," he moaned.

"No, this is something the Lord is doing. I don't know why yet, but He is in control. You've checked the oil every other time. There's a reason why you didn't this time. Don't worry, God has a plan."

Monday, he went to the garage. On his way, Walt Warkintin met him. "Bissell your van has to have a new motor. We're going to put it in and have it ready for next Saturday, and it isn't going to cost you one penny! You've done so much for Hume Lake, it's little enough that we can do for you."

Back in the cabin, he danced me around in his arms. "How'd you like to have a new motor, free?" He was delighted.

The week was excitingly full and free from worry. We went to get the van Saturday, expecting to visit our old home church, but it wasn't ready. "I guess the Lord wants us to stay up here for Sunday." We were very willing.

The services, dinner and a boat ride with loved ones was great. As the young people rowed the boat, Bissell said, "Let me have a hand at that. I haven't done it for years." He took over and when it was time to dock, he did it like a pro. Although his sight was failing, he strode down the pier pleased with himself that he could still steer well.

Don and Alice took us up to the cabin. He looked up at the jewelled sky. "Wouldn't it be wonderful if I could go right on up from here?"

He got a drink, read his Bible and went to bed. He awakened me around midnight. "What's the matter, Bissell. Don't you feel well?"

"Oh there's just a strange feeling around here," rubbing his chest. He went back to sleep. At seven o'clock, I heard labored breathing and I rushed to my missionary friend next door. Her brother rushed for the doctor and we ran back.

He was already with the Lord.

Loving friends took me to the French's cabin and made all the arrangements. News traveled like wildfire. Friends came from far and near. One man and wife that Bissell had taken to Sunday school when they were children, insisted on buying me a new outfit for the funeral. The Lord's hand was so evident in every detail; I felt His comfort and strength. Young people we had discipled in our home before we left for Ireland, came and sang. Now they were recording artists, serving the Lord and honoring the man who showed them how to walk as Jesus walked. Only the house Bissell Garrett tabernacled in for seventy-five years was laid to rest—he lives on in the many thousands of lives his godly life has touched.

When he retired and the Lord led him to sell out, he said, "We can't take our houses and lands to heaven with us, but we can take boys and girls." His investments are bringing dividends of immeasurable value for eternity.

CHAPTER 24

Aunt Birdies Comfort
A BLESSED REUNION SOME DAY

I still had that fifty-seven dollars as I headed back to central South Dakota alone. It was a long, lonely journey, but I still felt His hand comforting, providing for and protecting me. All funeral expenses were paid by loved ones. There was no more than gas money for the trip, so I slept in the van and fasted after I left Oregon and friends there.

Very tired and hungry, I pulled into the ranch just at six o'clock expecting a warm welcome and an invitation to sit down at the loaded table. Instead, the wife met me at the door.

"The key is under the cellar door. You won't have any electricity till you pay the meter. There's a little propane left in the tank. You can use that till it's gone, and then you'll have to pay for it to be filled. Good night." The door closed.

They claimed to be Christians and wanted a Christian teacher. I was stunned. No word of sympathy over the loss of my beloved husband. I unloaded alone, wept alone, moved the heavy piano and overstuffed furniture out of the way so I could get at my own things—alone. I cleaned and arranged the school alone—no, not really...the Lord was very near all the time.

They promised to take me to their church. I just knew they would treat me better when they got to know me. The seventeen-mile drive was one-sided as I tried to enter into their way of life. In the village church, I had to hunt to find a seat, near the front, next to the wall. They knew their lessons and the sermon was good. I stood near the pastor at the door as the people filed out, shaking his hand and telling him what a good message he had given, but not one soul took my proffered hand.

"I lead the junior choir, so you'll have to wait a while till we practice," the wife announced. I sat down. Finished, the pianist hurried to the door. "Heard you lost your husband. Sorry about that. My husband's waiting so I have to rush." She was gone.

In the months that followed, with all my efforts to break the ice, the clique remained an impenetrable fortress and I was outside.

"You needn't try to win those families to the Lord. You can't reach them with a ten-foot pole," I was advised by the rancher, speaking of the other families.

As the water truck filled the cistern, this lady who they said you couldn't talk to about the Lord stood by my car window an hour and shared her problems and heard God's answers. From then on, the women took turns coming for cousins, but hanging around to talk an hour or so.

"I see those women are bothering you after school. I'll put a stop to that," the rancher's wife insisted.

"Oh, please don't. I love having them visit. They tell me their troubles and I tell them the answers from God's Word. Don't you want them to come to know the Lord?"

"I don't believe it. They won't listen."

"But they really do," I insisted.

All that semester the rancher's children hurried home to noon dinner. As soon as they were out of sight, the cousins began asking questions and we'd have a good Bible study. They invited me to their homes and showed great love and interest.

I had to teach the county superintendent's courses and keep up with the schedule. The children worked hard during class, but the rancher's son never did his homework. He ran out of fingers to count on when in the fourth-grade math. I used the phone in the school to call the superintendent. "What do I do? Should I give him a low grade or an incomplete?" I asked her. "He works hard in school time, but he's never learned his tables." I had scarcely hung up when the father and his wife stormed in.

"You said one thing that is true: My son is smart enough. If he's behind it's your fault."

"He works hard during school time, but things he should have mastered in the first grade, he hasn't memorized, so he has to count on his fingers."

"Make him stay in at recess."

"He's an active boy. I can't ask him to sit at a desk all day. He needs exercise. He never does the homework I assign."

If angry words could kill, I'd have been dead. As they left, I quietly said, "Thank you for coming. Now I know better what to expect. I want to help him all I can." The mother was surprised at my soft answer.

I understood what folks meant when they said if I didn't hit it off with Mr. H., I'd never make it. The former teacher had been partial and had given unearned grades to please him, but it cheated the children.

"Don't try to teach those other kids. They'll never amount to anything except raising hogs. You give your time to helping mine," he demanded.

"I have to live with myself. I can't be partial nor give unearned grades," I replied.

After each tongue lashing, I would be so upset that I couldn't sleep. My heart would beat so hard it shook the bed. The little girl's parents were deeply concerned for my welfare. "If you can get word to us, we'll take you to a doctor any hour, day or night."

I trained the children for a Christmas program that was suited to their abilities and needs. I had purchased a little chord organ at a teachers' convention and taught them some carols.

"Are those women coming to your program?" the ranch wife asked.

"Of course! They wouldn't miss it!"

"Well, I guess we'll have to come in self defense!"

We had costumes, lighting effects and the beautiful story of Jesus' birth and purpose for hanging on the cross to pay for our sins. The cousins had gone the thirty-six miles into Winner and purchased lovely gifts for me that included the Word of God. In contrast, the "rich rancher" gave a little scale to weigh letters that may have cost a dollar.

"If you can find anyone who can teach your children better to your liking," I informed him, "I'll gladly resign and not take any pay I haven't earned."

He agreed until he learned the daughter of one he hated had applied for the school. "You're under contract. You can't leave." He changed his tune.

"I'll do the best I can if you want me to finish the year."

I left for Lincoln to spend the holidays with my sister. With no tax and less cost, I stocked up on food supplies. With grocery stores thirty-six miles away and blizzards, it was wise to stock up on food. When I had first come, I had no money or a chance to go to town till my September check, so I ate cucumbers and string beans. They had a surplus of these so for two months this was my main diet.

When I got back, the former teachers had finally moved their stuff out and, at last, I was able to arrange my things and feel at home. Then came a knock; the rancher and a board member announced they had found a young man in a teachers' college who was willing to drop out and finish the year.

After the momentary shock, I calmly smiled, "That's just fine. I hope he will do well and be happy."

"I want you to take everything out of here in a day or two," he demanded, "and your library out of the school. That took away their interest in their lessons."

"Wouldn't you like to have me leave a bed and dishes to meet this young man's needs?"

"No, he has to fend for himself."

I called the pastor who had been a board member for the Boy's Ranch. He came from Winner with a team of workers and trucks and they cleared out in a few hours. As neighbors drove past the ranch, they aimed a thumb toward the house. "Do you think they are real Christians?"

"That's between them and the Lord," I replied. There, in the parsonage, I was instantly included as family and loved by all. As the pastor sang "Jesus The Son of God" with the voice of an angel, the pent-up feelings broke lose, and I sobbed till my heart was returned to its normal rhythm.

All my furniture was just what another pastor needed. He and his wife had lost everything by their stay in a hospital, so they welcomed the things I would need no more. I stayed a while with the son of these dear ones who met my need, so they could attend a conference. Then, we loaded my van and I headed for Lincoln, Nebraska. The news said roads were all clear. That was true in South Dakota, but the roads on the Nebraska side were solid sheets of ice. Most hills and curves had been sanded, so I slowly made progress. But, suddenly, there was no sand and a strong sidewind. Making a U-turn that was unplanned, the van landed on its side beside the icy road. I hadn't put my seat belt on, so I dropped to the bottom; it looked much wider to that window beyond the steering wheel. It was hard to climb up to look out.

Some young men came to my rescue. They thought I was bleeding. Friends had given me a glass of jelly just before leaving—that is a spread. It broke and spread red all over my face and hair. I was a sweet mess!

They took me to town, and I washed up as best I could and returned with the wrecker. "There goes my last paycheck," I moaned. I was hoping to save it for the mission field.

This man was different than my former experiences with wreckers. He was as gentle as a nurse and set the van up so skillfully that almost nothing was broken. The side was caved in four inches, but the pastor used jacks and restored it to its proper place.

I reached Lincoln in the middle of the night. My nephew's mother, who was expecting me, was waiting. She had to help me out of the car and through a bath and to bed.

"What was happening to you at three o'clock this afternoon?" she wanted to know.

"That was the time I tipped over."

"The Lord told me you were in danger, so I called Nonie and we prayed for you." That's why the men, the wrecker and the Lord were so good to me. After three days in bed, I was ready to return to help the pastor and bring the rest of my possessions to Lincoln. On that trip, the generator gave out and my lights went out after I got on the main highway. A kind lady dared to stop and call my nephew who came with a fresh battery to get me to their home safely.

The highway to Heaven has some steep and difficult places. We wonder why there is all the pain of those months in the lonely prairies, but we go on by faith, knowing God has an ultimate intention for each trial.

Before the next year was ended, He revealed one reason why I was sent: The dear little girl went into the arms of Jesus through the door of Leukemia. No doubt others—they who professed, but didn't possess the Savior and had said they couldn't be touched with a ten-foot pole—found entrance through the embrace of loving arms.

CHAPTER 25

Assignment By Command
State Home for children

"You are always interested in needy children," my sister stated.

"The state home for children is very near. They are constantly in need of house parents. Why don't you go and apply?"

As I sat in the waiting room, the secretary came out of her office. "Mrs. Garrett!" She was glad to see me. We had prayed together the night before at church. "I'm so glad you're applying. We need you! This was a Christian orphanage till the State took it over; they got rid of the praying Christians. There are only three left who pray for those needy kids." She was rejoicing that I would share their burden. "There's another missionary here who had a children's home in Ireland. Do you know her?"

My heart nearly stopped. She was the last person in the world I ever wanted to see again. Our first year in Avoca Manor with the sixteen little ones, she caused us more work and trials than all the children. When we were introduced to the new assignment, the field director said she would only stay a month. She hadn't come as an approved member of our mission, but, when she left another mission, he felt sorry for her and gave her a temporary job. Her month became twelve at our personal expense, for she contributed nothing but chaos.

"If she's working here I don't think I want to take the job."

"Oh, please stay. She isn't very well thought of here, and we need you so much," she begged.

Just then, the personnel officer invited me into her office. "I just overheard you were a missionary in Ireland. Do you know Ellie Kay?"

"Yes, I know her very well."

"Will you tell me if this application she signed is true?" She pulled out the statement of qualifications. "She says here that she was matron of a children's home in Eire for five years and had the total responsibility for thirty-two children. Is that true?"

"No, not a word of it is true. She came to help in a Rescue Mission in Dublin, but she caused it to close. She was so bossy none of the girls would stay. One of the founders died soon after, brokenhearted. She told a pitiful story of how she'd had a nervous breakdown because she had been so overworked. The field director believed her lies and let her stay at the home for sixteen school-age children, but staff resigned because of her. So his wife took her to help with the sixteen babies, but, when they had to go, we inherited her. She wasn't in Ireland that long and at no time was she in charge of a single child."

"I thought so," the officer replied. "She got in here because of influential relations. We've tried her in several departments and she makes a mess of everything she does."

"That's the way she was in the home. She was more trouble than all the children. She stole things form our apartment and ate the candy given to the children.

"That's what she does here. She comes into my office and helps herself."

"My husband refused to let her return to the home when she came back without permission from headquarters. She expected to sponge off of us again. The field director said, 'What shall I do? If I send her right back, she could blackmail us.' he moaned.

"'You're the director,' Bissell replied. 'We're through supporting her. Because my wife wouldn't fight for her rights, she treated her like a cat who has a mouse cornered. If she comes—we go.'

"He ended up taking her to look after two girls at Drewstown House who were slow-minded, but the Lord answered prayer. When she went to the doctor, he told her this climate was too damp for her and soon she'd have crippling arthritis. So she returned to Lincoln. There, she talked the Christian Business Women into paying her way for a nice Florida vacation. I've had all I can take of her. I don't think I want to take the job."

"Oh, please do. We need you so badly. I'll promise, you won't have any trouble with her," she pleaded.

"I'll have to pray about it." I left remembering that stress-filled year, her attempt to return without permission and then, when she left, how the Drewston folks who had received so much from us started treating us as if we had leprosy. For the next year and a half, we were treated shamefully. Bissell wanted to just stay far from the mission headquarters, but I said, "I don't know what has caused this rejection, but, whatever it was, I feel I should face it and so live that our good name will be accepted." He cooperated, humbly.

We moved to Oregon and I taught in the Christian school run by the World Mission to Children the next year. Toward the end of the school year, one of the women who was kind and helped gather wild herbs to make our $25.00-a-month support stretch, listened as I started telling her about the painful experiences we had with Ella.

"I don't know why I'm telling you this," I had been very close-mouthed about all the problems we experienced in Ireland. "But I feel impelled to share this with you.

"You've always had this problem," she interrupted.

"What problem?"

"Oh, you know."

"No, I don't know what you are talking about, but I want to."

"You're a homosexual," she replied. "Ella told us."

"So that's her revenge for not letting her return. Did you ever hear of a homosexual being happily married for fourteen years without a single quarrel?"

"Well, I never thought of that," she mused. "Oh, I'm so glad it isn't true." Gradually, those who scorned us began to become friends again; but when my former missionary partner and her husband were hospitalized by a car crash, we went to their rescue in the heart of South Dakota.

Helping with DVBS and camps for ranchers and Indians, Uncle Bissell began to respond to their love. He had been like a man in his prime until we were forced to leave the children we loved as much as if they were our own. When we had to leave them to strangers, he aged very rapidly, felt his work was finished and wished God would take him home.

The new project to save homeless boys needed a teacher and caretaker, so, for the next nine months, we helped with Hillcrest For Boys. The head of welfare would have given us up to three hundred boys and all their support if we left the Christian emphasis out of our program.

That year, we had only three boys; but to rescue them was worth the hard work and blizzards. Besides, the military housing had many children who spent all their free time with us. So it was worthwhile.

I worked hard. Days were fine, I enjoyed the boys; but at night, I couldn't sleep well for the next two years.

The sacrifice of all our property to meet the needs of the two homes in Eire was nothing, but the loss of our good name was devastating. A little demon of resentment would show his gleaming eyes and tantalize me with thoughts of how our patient endurance and support had been rewarded by a forked tongue. I would forgive, bury the hurtful thoughts and try to sleep; but there it was springing right back out of the grave to add bitterness to my aching heart.

Here I was, of all places, being asked to work in the same institution again. I fought against it, but the Lord kept saying, "This thing is from me. Trust me. I will go with you through this trial."

🦜 🦜 🦜

Elly was on vacation when I started work there. I was substituting in all departments and, by the time she returned, I had gained the love of all the children and staff. I was walking up the ramp from the office when she returned. When she saw me, she nearly fainted. When she regained her composure, she put on an act as if glad to see me and asked to borrow my slides of the children in the home in Ireland. The personnel officer came out and said, "I wouldn't loan my slides to my own sister." Elly kept pestering me because she wanted to show them and speak to the Christian Business Women's Club. Finally, I said I would bring my slides and show them and she could do the talking. That ended her little plan.

At Christmas time, I was blessed with many tokens of love that the children wanted to express. I met Elly in the hall. She looked me in the eye, "I didn't get one single gift this Christmas." She looked so pitiful my heart melted.

"Oh, you poor, deluded soul. You tried to grab for all you could get by clever lies and manipulation, and you've lost everything of value."

That did it. The demon left never to return. All I kept in my heart was pity that led to prayer for her, I think, finally, the Lord led her out of her darkness and into Christian work.

My eighteen months in the State home were eventful and sometimes exciting. As a relief parent, I went around to every department as the regular couples had days off and vacations. My first day kept me humping for twenty-four hours. Many were sick and no one was there to fill the gaps. So I had reception, infirmary, night phone calls, and had to get many ready for doctor and dentist appointments.

Next day I was sent to the intensive-care ward. I met two heavy-set black girls, a street-wise blonde and a thirteen-year-old who was deranged. The house parents told me later that they planned to give me a bad time—coming in alone. But I wasn't alone. They just couldn't see Jesus with me. Right off, they accused Lou Ann of breaking the television set and were going to beat up on her. She screamed a denial. I knew better than to tackle the three big teens, so I held Lou Ann's arms behind her back and shut the door to her room behind her. She beat the door and screamed till it could be heard all over the campus.

I quietly asked one of the girls to go after a man to calm her down. As I tucked each girl in bed, I knelt at their cot and prayed for them. They never got around to the deviltry they had planned.

When Lou Ann wouldn't go to school the next day, I sent her to her room, so she went to school. From then on, all responded to personal attention and love. Years later, Lou Ann wrote and said, "Please come back. No one else loves us like you did."

Cottage Number One was made up of sixteen of the oldest boys. A young man from Wesleyan University was to be my helper for a month of the summer. I was amused when he offered to loan me any of his books on religion or answer any of my questions. He had just graduated and had all the answers. By the second day, he was sitting on the kitchen counter asking me for answers. We got on fine. Those boys were with me, too.

When I got my assignment and knew how destructive those boys had been—sometimes a threat to house parents' lives—I prayed. The Lord led me to get a form of a bust and cover it with modeling clay. It was a life-size head ready to work on. "I've always wanted to make a bust of a typical black boy," I announced. "Would you be my model, Butch?" I turned to the most feared young man in the home. Daily, he posed as I made it like the prize-fighter type he was. No one dared cross me because I was his friend. Sometimes he would come to my bed and kneel to pray with me. When he graduated, I presented his likeness—brown color and all—in plaster of Paris. It was on display in the front hall when I left.

🍂 🍂 🍂

At the time when Communists were inciting blacks to go on riots, Rickey was among the kids who were caught. He was brought in while I was in reception. After processing him, I tucked him in bed, and, as I always did, I asked in a cheery voice, "Would you like me to pray for you tonight?" They were free to say yes or no. It was OK.

I had a retarded boy of eight, Eugene, who was a permanent resident of reception, for no one else wanted him. Rickey had been taught to hate anyone who was white. Eugene was white and so was I. Rickey would be mean to him every chance he got, so I had to protect him. Then he started singing a filthy song blaspheming the Lord Jesus. As I prayed for him, I told him I loved the Lord Jesus and it must make Him very sad to hear His name used in such a bad way.

He took that as a challenge and told the others to sing it with him or he would beat them up. When I would come in sight, they would start their song. I became deaf and ignored them, but made over them when they were good. Soon, it wasn't fun when I said nothing.

One day, Eugene was playing in the dirt a little way from me. Rickey streaked through the yard like a black panther to beat up Eugene before I could rescue him. He was put in the intensive care ward, so I didn't see him for some time. Then, that house father died and the boys were shifted around.

I was back at reception. I took my boys to the indoor pool. Eugene had been naughty so he couldn't go in. When the lifeguard disappeared Rickey and a black friend raced to the shallow end, grabbed him and were about to throw him in the deep end when the guard rescued him. We sat and watched as far as we could from the shallow end. Again, when the guard disappeared, Rickey rushed at him and began beating him. My Irish anger flared. I pounded with my fists on his back. "You great big bully. You ought to be ashamed of yourself, beating up on a little guy like that.

Surprised, he growled, "You hit me!"

"Yes, I hit you. I'll hit you again if you ever attack this little guy."

With the swiftness of a bullet, his elbow flew back and cracked the bone in my arm. At that moment, the guard appeared and ordered him out of the pool. As my boys went to dress, they said Rickey was in there. The guard had seen him leave, but somehow he had come back. As he was personally ushered out the door, he clenched his fist as he passed me, "I'll get you!"

I called his house parents, "I'd like an escort to reception. Rickey has threatened to get me." We waited and waited.

Finally, the house mother came. "My husband has him in tow now. You can go back."

I got off duty in reception at nine o'clock and went through a door into the infirmary. Since no girls were in that room, I went to sleep next to the open door so I could hear any boy needing help or the night phone calls. Next morning, I went through that open door—there was Rickey. Our heads had been inches apart as we slept.

The house parent had called the case worker and demanded Rickey be removed. He'd had all he could take. So the case worker put him to bed in my department.

The young fellows in Number One had gone on a "blow." The "psychologist" recommended that they be allowed to curse and swear and destroy property "to let off the anger inside." They just got worse. No one wanted that cottage. They hired a huge, black football player from the university to come. He refused to do any work so they had to hire a cleaning woman and cook. They told the boys they shouldn't go to church—we were coercing them! After a few weeks, they were taking large quantities from the store to give their friends. Finally, they were fired.

The superintendent came to me as I was going off duty in reception. "Will you come and help me?" he pleaded. "They've done around $35,000 worth of damage on that cottage, and no one will take over. If you'll come, I'll stay with you."

"It would have been a lot easier if you had put me over there when the boys asked for me, when their house father died. They're on such a high now, it'll be hard to settle them down."

Like the calm on the Sea of Galilee when Jesus said, "Peace, be still," the boys began to quiet down. Big, black Arthur piped up, "Aunt Birdie, will you pray for me tonight?"

"I sure will and any of the rest of you who want me to. Now it's late. Let's get to bed." They quietly went off to their rooms. The superintendent also disappeared.

The night watchman came to the door. "What has he done, leaving you in this place alone."

"I'm not alone, I have the Lord. I'll be OK."

"When you get all these wild animals in their cage, you go to your room, shut the door and lock it; and, even if they tear the place up, don't go out. I'll be watching all night. If you have trouble, flash the light off and on and I'll come with help."

I thanked him. I knew why he had such fear for me. The brother of one of them had asked his wife for the car keys. When she turned to call her husband to make sure he had sent him, he had picked up a butcher knife and killed her.

As I went from room to room, all but two welcomed the prayer time on my knees holding hands. That pair was afraid of being teased.

The last room was Arthur's. After I prayed, I turned to his roommate. "Rickey, would you like me to pray for you tonight?" I gripped his hand and put my head near his heart and prayed.

As I started to close my door, I stopped. No! I'll not close my door. They'll think I'm afraid of them. Lord I just ask you to send an angel to be my door keeper. I went to sleep trusting in Him.

The next day was Saturday. Every boy got up and did chores and went off to sports. I did the housework and prepared the meals.

"Now tomorrow, if all you boys go to church, I can go, too. If it's all right, we'll have lunch at noon and dinner in the evening, OK?" I had a Volkswagen van with an open top and had taken them to parks, etc., letting them look out the top and yell all they liked.

Saturday, as I made the rounds to pray, the last room held Arthur and Rickey. The burden for those boys overwhelmed me, and I burst into tears as I knelt by Arthur and held him close. Struggling to regain my composure, I knelt by Rickey and took his hand in mine. Sobbing, I cried, "Oh God, maybe no one has ever cared whether this boy lives or dies, but I do. I don't want him to go on the way he is and go to hell."

His hands gripped mine with a vice grip. I felt God was speaking to his heart. My head rested near his heart.

Next morning, every boy got clean and dressed for church. Rickey went to mass and my van was packed. All seemed happy to go to my little church. I was proud of them—so well behaved.

After lunch, while the dishes were being washed, Rickey approached me, "Aunt Birdie, could I have a talk with you in private...alone?"

"Sure, Rickey, come on in my room." I closed the door and I locked it. The other boys stopped to listen. They all feared him, except me. That tall, tough teenager looked into my eyes. "You know that prayer you said last night. I can't get away from it. I don't want to go on the way I am and be a thief and go to hell." He burst into tears. We wept together on each others shoulders. Then we knelt by my bed and I told him the wonderful story of the Savior who died on the cross to pay for all his sins. I believe the angels rejoiced that day over a sinner saved by grace.

Until I left for Colombia, Rickey and Arthur were my shadow when they were free to be with me. As my van rolled away, they waved until I was out of sight, but they remained in my heart.

After my short term in Colombia, I returned and married Frank McKimens. Fifteen years later, we went to Lincoln for my sister's fiftieth anniversary. I phoned the prayer partners from the home.

"Oh, I'm so glad you called," the teacher was elated. "Arthur just called from back east and asked if I knew where Aunt Birdie was. He left his number and asked me to tell you he still loves the Lord and wants you to know."

"Do you know where Rickey is?" I wondered.

"I'll try to find out." She told of Keith and others who were doing fine, those who often sought special prayers. The phone rang. Rickey was excited and wanted me to come right over. It wasn't far. He was head house parent for two halfway homes now. I told him I'd be there as soon as I could. He was waiting on the porch and ran out to meet me. Now he was a grown man, but the boy that once hated whites now threw his arms around me. He told me how the Lord had helped him live a straight life so that he had a good job and even a position in a bank—he who was a thief before he met Jesus.

I told him of the story of Jesus who had a hundred sheep, but one got lost and He went after it. "And I was that little black sheep," he rejoiced.

"I'm glad you're talking to him about God," the assistant on duty said. "I've been trying to get him to read this book and he won't." He held up a Jehovah's Witness text. Rickey explained, "I don't want to read that. I think I better stick with just the Bible."

"Let's go out to the car where we can pray," I suggested. When we were alone, I asked, "If you had a jar of honey and slipped in some lead arsenic and you had another jar full of lead arsenic, which would be the most dangerous to have around?"

"I suppose the jar of honey," he figured.

"That's the way the cults attract you. They offer you honey with just enough error or poison in it to send you to hell. You're right to stick to the Bible."

Fellowship is a foretaste of heaven. When we get there, we won't have to say good-bye and trust God to send others to lead the babes in Christ on to maturity.

❧ ❧ ❧

Quite a population in the home were Indians. They are clannish. If you make one an enemy, you have the rest bucking you, too. At one home, a house father slapped an Indian girl for her impudence. Her brother and gang demanded he come out so they could kill him. The couple left under police protection for a forced vacation till the boys cooled down. It gave the impression that the boys were right and the parents were the ones to be penalized.

I was on duty when these Indian girls were in restricted freedom. The one who was slapped was the leader of the girls' gang. As I tucked each one in bed that night, I knelt by her pal's bed and prayed. Tears began to flow; my heart ached for those misplaced children. Try as I would, I could not keep the tears back. They are so stoic, they'll think I'm weak, I thought. But, to my surprise, the tough ringleader reached out as I knelt beside her to pray and drew my head next to her heart, and I felt love flowing in.

In the next dorm, the girls began to ask me about the Lord and how they could be saved. Lights were out and we talked in low tones. I heard bare feet slipping into the room. Those Indian girls wanted to hear, too. From then on all the Indians were my special friends.

It seemed we who cared for these souls were in such a minority that there was little hope of a happy ending in their lives. Many of their parents were in jail or so bound by sin, their children were not wanted. What hope could we offer them?

The case workers were taught the kids should be allowed to release pent-up feelings by doing what came naturally. An overstuffed psychiatrist sat in an overstuffed chair in the conference room puffing a big cigar and, for sixty dollars an hour, he counselled the staff to let them go on a blow, throwing rocks through dorm windows, etc.; the government would replace them. When girls climbed out the windows to meet their boyfriends for sex, we should look the other way. Sex pressure had to be satisfied some way. He explained that his wife got so that she didn't meet his needs, so he divorced her and got a young girl the age of his daughter to satisfy him.

One of the house parents piped up, "Then you are saying that we should run a house of prostitution?"

"Well, I wouldn't call it that," he responded. "We must be tolerant and try to meet their needs."

CHAPTER 26

About Beautiful Colombia

The missionary couple in front of me at the prayer meeting were asking prayer for much-needed teachers in their Christian academy.

"I'm a teacher," I responded.

"When can we talk to you?" they turned around excitedly. That started the ball rolling on the course to Colombia under Gospel Missionary Union. I went through orientation and was dedicated for a two-year term just before my sixtieth birthday. Since I was taking school supplies as well as my own, and veteran missionary Avis Van Egdom was going with me, we steamed out of New Orleans on my birthday.

It seemed that eight, the number of new beginnings was significant in my life. Born on the twenty-eighth day of the eighth month in 1908, and each decade-year something special took place. After graduating from Biola, my first commissioning was on my fortieth. Bissell and I were commissioned for my first foreign field on my fiftieth, On my sixtieth, to Colombia, and seventieth, my Bible classes met in the Crown Room at King City for a potluck dinner and viewing of slides of my life story. I got back from a summer with SEND International in Alaska to speak at my home church and enjoyed a beautiful cake and fellowship with loved ones on my eightieth. I'm looking forward to my ninetieth here or there—or in the air.

Back to the story.

Avis had been in Colombia through the five years called the "Blood Bath," when the wealthy bureaucracy of the Roman Church saw that they were losing members and money because the peasants had been so robbed they were turning to the Communists—who offered them material gain—or to the Christians—who offered persecution now, but eternal rewards in Heaven. They declared war on both groups, killed many Christians and destroyed churches. Avis lost her husband and returned to the states to put her son through school. After we shared in his graduation and he went to Africa as a missionary, we went on to Colombia together. What a blessing she was—lovingly helping this novice in the culture and difficulties of adjustments.

As we sat at table on the freighter, a young man across from me asked about my purpose in going.

"So, you're a missionary!" He had a sneer on his face. "Well, let me tell you, Christianity doesn't work. It's been tried for two thousand years and what has been gained? I've been five years studying in Notre Dame University and I've decided that Communism is the answer. I come from a wealthy family in Peru and we have haciendas and banks in our name. It would cost me everything I own, but, if it will make a better world, I'm willing to give it all up for the cause."

"But you haven't been introduced to genuine Christianity." For the three-days journey through the Panama Canal and on to Buena Ventura, we spent many hours discussing our goals. At first, he wanted to argue, but then began to listen intently. The last evening, we sat on deck till the wee hours. He dug out his Catholic Bible and compared with mine.

"Yes, it does say the same…just like you said," he marveled. Light was beginning to dawn in his troubled heart. He spent time with us while the ship was unloading until the time for him to go on to Peru. I continued to pray for him and trust I'll meet him in Heaven because God promised that if He began a good work in someone's heart, He would finish it.

A GMU missionary came to help us through customs, a three-day ordeal. Even though we watched, things disappeared. The missionary rode on the truck with our many boxes while Avis and I squeezed into a taxi to go over the coastal range. A full moon made tropical mountain grandeur look ethereal, as puffs of white clouds reflected the moon on dark backdrops.

We stopped. The driver told us to roll up our windows. We obeyed even though it was hot. Then, when he drove right through a waterfall, we understood why. He ignored all rules of safety as we rushed over crooked, narrow roads. Trucks didn't pull off the road for a rest stop. He just drove around them. We didn't relax until we came to a stop in the main plaza in Cali and the field director was there to meet us. Two of their daughters would be my students.

The next day, I was taken to Lianita, a village in the foothills of the Andes. When they left me at the teacherage, they hurried away and only the pastors of village churches were there, and they knew no English. I got out my Spanish-English dictionary and we tried, with laughter, to communicate. My little fun thing that is an "ice breaker" in getting acquainted with boys that always brings a laugh is the "milk man's" handshake; where you have them put fingers together, turn them upside down, and the thumbs make good udders to "milk." The two men doubled up with laughter. The local pastor was living on the compound and milked the cows and maintained the grounds. The language barrier didn't keep them from being my close friends.

His wife showed how cocoa, coffee and sugar cane were processed for use. Many times she would bring me orchids when I needed encouragement. When she nearly cut her thumb off, she refused to go to the doctor forty-six miles away, but came to me to clean out the gaping cut that they had packed with whitewash to stop the bleeding. With no pain killer, I had to clean out the lime, pull it together and dress it with my first-aid equipment. She'd rather have the love and pain than the expertise of a professional.

When the heavy boxes of school supplies and my things arrived, we found the case with all my good clothing had disappeared on the way over the mountains when the missionary had gone into a cafe for a snack. But, the Lord had permitted that loss for my gain. As I had packed at HQ, they offered me a little refrigerator someone had left. I had discarded my old clothes as not worth the space, but here was an empty fridge, so I stuffed them in. That was what I wore for two years; that made me one with the poor. They would idolize the well-dressed missionaries, but I was poor like them and not fluent in Spanish so they could teach me.

I had only eight students. One was sharp little Ann, who was pre-K and spent all her time in the school room absorbing the recitations. All were in different grades and some had special problems. Two Colombians had to learn English as well. One girl was in eighth grade and couldn't do fourth-grade work because she had never been made to study if she didn't want to, and she didn't have a "want to." Her folks expected me to prepare her for high school in one year. She wouldn't even try.

Another was a precious boy whose dad compared him to his quick-witted younger brother. Chuck was talented in crafts and thorough in his work. He made remarkable progress when he felt loved and encouraged.

Sharon Harder had just graduated from Grace Bible Institute and came as my helper to see if she could adjust to a foreign mission field. We worked together very well; while I took each student to recite or counsel, she would supervise the rest.

At first, she would lock her door and window, but, as she saw that I opened up for the evening cool and trusted the Lord for safety, she became sure of His watch care, too. She went on for further training and has been a valuable witness for our Lord in Bogota for many years.

For my birthday, the children gave me a young parrot. Lorenzo was a real pet. He rode around on the tractor or bikes or shoulders. When the dog had puppies, he was right there to investigate. I rigged up a place to swing, play and perch over my sink. He would be on his perch through the night, but as soon as he heard me stir, he would fly down. I'd hear the claws click on the tile floors and, with beak and feet, he'd climb up the bedding and cuddle. He'd turn upside down for me to scratch his tummy. If he had to "go," he'd perch on the foot of my bed to leave his droppings. When I was gone on the few vacations and others took care of him, he'd cry like a baby. When I got back, he didn't want me out of his sight.

The second year was more difficult than the first as I had no helper and twenty-three classes a day, plus swimming and doing the janitor's work. Because they planned on closing the academy the next year, the supplies were inadequate. If I had a text, there wasn't a workbook or answer book to match. I had never had New Math, but I had to teach it in all classes. I didn't have answers ready made, and it took lots of preparation.

One of the Colombian missionaries returned from a period of sick leave and desired the teaching job. She thought it was easy to teach eight children. So, I offered to resign. The three Colombian children were preparing to go to Mexico and Ann was taken out of kindergarten, so she had only five to teach.

I became governess for an adopted Colombian. His mother had died, and the father hired nationals who did not discipline. At times, Kevin was a terror at first, but, as I played boy fun with him and the dogs and my parrot, we became pals. At night, he would climb in bed with me and listen to stories until sleep overtook him. As he came to understand the love of the Lord, he became my interpreter as I explained the gospel to the cook and gardener.

When his father was called to the orient on business, I took him to his grandparents. On the flight, he anxiously urged me to again explain the gospel and he asked Jesus to be his Savior. The last news I had of him was good.

I went on to the Gospel Missionary Union in Kansas to report and get my Volkswagen van which I had loaned them. It hadn't had good care and I had to pay for repairs and paint. I got to the edge of South Dakota and it broke down. I phoned Audrey, my missionary partner who was now Mrs. Badgett and now lived on the north edge. Vernon just happened to be visiting near where I was. He hadn't been in that area for many months. He towed my car to their home. I bought a new motor which he installed and I paid what they owed on a Dodge van he had made into an all-weather camper.

The mission they had served for many years took in some liberal men at headquarters who demanded that they compromise Biblical principles; so they resigned, which meant all their equipment—including a bus—went to the mission. They took a small church with little support.

The Colombian family who wanted to travel with me to the West, suddenly changed their plans. I had arranged meetings in the western states where I was well-known, and they had planned to accompany me.

CHAPTER 27

Always Believe Christ
AN INTRODUCTION TO FRANK MCKIMENS

The first year Audrey and I were with Youth Home Missions we were often in lumber towns. Canby, California, was one village where many hearts were touched.

A dear couple was burdened for Frank. He was marrying Esther, who was a fine Christian and believed Frank was, too; but the men at the mill knew he wasn't. So they invited us to a delicious dinner and when Frank started off, I followed him to the gate.

"Do you know the difference between a professing Christian and a possessing Christian?"

He didn't. I explained that getting sprinkled as a baby, Church membership and spending an hour in church each week does not make anyone a possessing Christian. He promised he would read the New Testament daily and pray that God would open his heart to the truth. He kept his promise. When he reached 1 John 1:9, "If we confess our sins, He is faithful and just to forgive us our sins and to cleanse us from all unrighteousness," he exclaimed, "That's for me." For Frank, who would never admit he was wrong, God used that to cause him to confess he was a sinner and seek forgiveness. After that experience, he expected everyone else to be saved the same way.

When Bissell and I returned from Ireland, we became house parents one summer for the mission school in Grants Pass. We used some of my war bonds for the down payment on a little rundown house near the campus. While the children were in school, I painted and fixed it up. Frank and Esther brought venison and food from their big garden for the mission and thanked me for leading him to Christ. When we moved in, they gave us many things we needed. I taught through the school year, then rented it to a family who wanted their children in a Christian school. (One of them has been in Africa many fruitful years. She and her husband are Wycliff Bible translators.) As school closed we were called up to South Dakota to help Audrey and Ike Badgett.

Having no place to store the pretty dishes and such that were my wedding presents, I took them to Esther, "If I never get back, you can have them." They were going over plans for a new home in King City. Their nice home in Central Point was ideal for a filling station, so it was sold for a good price.

"Let me have a look at those plans. I have always been interested in efficiency." They followed my suggestions. I never dreamed I would be using that home for 30 years after Esther moved into her heavenly home. Frank continued corresponding after Esther died. When he asked me to come and marry him, I had no desire to marry again—I still loved the man who gave me his name.

I had been self-supporting during the years with GMU. If I continued in Colombia, I had to take a job. Three offers to teach were extended, but I did not get an OK from God. It seemed He was urging me to say yes to Frank. He told me he was serving the Lord and loved Him with all his heart. As I prayed and sought God's directive will, He said, "This is the way. Walk ye in it."

Frank phoned while I was with Audrey. Since I had to do all the travelling alone, he begged me to get married right away so he could travel with me. If I had known what I was getting into, my story would have ended here.

But, God had His plan.

I was anxious to have the wedding in the chapel that had been very dear to us. I felt those of the mission who had believed the slander, started by the young woman when Bissell refused to let her sponge off of us another year, would be cleared up. She returned to Ireland without meeting the requirements. When she was not permitted to stay at the mission her excuse for returning to the U.S. was that I was a homosexual. By marrying Frank, who was well-liked by the mission, I felt that gossip would be squelched for good.

But after the knot was tied, I found the reality far from the image he had presented. The first night I cried out, "Oh, Lord. What have I done?" It was some time before I learned he had had a fever that should have killed him. The VA put him on drugs to slow him down and, after many threatening experiences, I learned he had Alzheimer's. Friends urged me to get an annulment, but I told them I had made a promise "for better or for worse." If I fade out, how can I advise young married couples to stick it out and trust the Lord to blend two strong wills into His will. He was a diamond in the rough, and life the first few years was very rough.

He wanted to travel all the time as long as I had the camper. I couldn't go anywhere without him, even to shop. If I put something in the cart, he would put it back; but I would go and pick it up and put it in the cart again. He wouldn't let me have my keys, saying I might lose them, as well as no money. He was in charge. There were times in despair I would walk the streets of King City after he was asleep and cry out, "Oh God, If I had those keys, I would take my van and go as far as I could and never come back." But, at last, I would humbly crawl in bed and pray for a better day.

My dear mother, who had such a hard marriage, would say, "When you get the worst of it, you make the best of it." She looked for the beauty in every situation and the good in every person. Following her example, I concentrated on the beautiful sights and lovable people in all our journeys.

Hunting season was a nightmare. We went hundreds of miles to mountainous areas where deer should be, and he would take off into the wild woods. Eventually, he would find his way back and impatiently make me go to another area.

Once, while high in the mountains, we had parked the camper in a canyon and hiked around four miles. He refused to let me carry a flashlight and matches. I realized we could never find our way back before dark. I saw a trail far below so I took off and he had to follow. God sent a pickup along just as we got to the road. He took us back to our van in the dark. We would never have made it. A doctor got separated from his son in that area that night and froze to death.

The next hunting season, we went to Europe to get a Volkswagen at the factory. We visited the Scandinavian countries, Europe, and that Christmas was enjoyed with the children in Ireland. They were now teens and it was the last time to be together. We had boxes of chocolate-covered raisins and gifts for both homes. God got them delivered with no excess-baggage cost.

CHAPTER 28

Adventures Beyond Comprehension

One summer, we drove to Alaska to help at Victory Bible Camp under Arctic Missions. The memories of those months would make fascinating stories, but the 18 years I had with Frank were some of God's refining fires. Out of the crucible, He was able to bring out the pure gold to offer our Lord. Through the many tests, God was able to develop love in Frank's heart for Jesus and for others. I could never help people with marital problems when I had Bissell, but many seek counsel since I learned to live with Frank.

I could write another book about the trials and the fruitful results in many lives as the Lord led us along the High Way. He had been afflicted with Algheimer's disorder the last 20 years of his 94½ years. He was so strong and determined that we knew God protected us. As Frank was regaining consciousness after a second operation, he heard my voice and lifted his arms toward heaven and exclaimed, "Beautiful! Isn't it beautiful?" From then on, until God took the last chip off the diamond, he was their favorite patient—thankful and loving to all. Like Bissell, when God was ready, he was awakened to meet his Savior in Heaven. Mission accomplished, I was anxious to go back to regions beyond where laborers are few.

Soon I was called back to Alaska for the summer and then on to Guam and the Micronesian Islands for the next seven years. Missionaries used my home rent-free for taking care of it.

If I ever get time, I would love to add those thrilling stories to another book of adventures the Lord had for me.

Now that He has made it necessary for me to return to my home in King City, part of my heart is left with the dear ones who learned to know my Lord and His precious Word through me. But, I'm still His missionary. Since I can't go to them, many call, write or visit; and prayer goes to the Throne of Grace just as well from here as from the far-flung mission fields where I've been.

I can honestly agree with David:

Delight yourself in the Lord; And He shall give you the desires of your heart. Commit your way to the Lord, Trust also in Him, and He shall bring it to pass." (Psalms 37:4–5)

I have been young and now I'm old; Yet I have not seen the righteous forsaken. (Psalms 37:25)

They shall bear fruit in old age. They shall be fresh and flourishing to declare that the Lord is upright. (Psalms 92:14)

They who wait upon the Lord will gain new strength; they will mount up with wings like eagles, they shall run and not get tired, they will walk and not become weary. (Isa. 40:31)

To order additional copies of

Aunt Birdie's Chronicles

please send $10.00
plus $3.95 shipping and handling to:

Juanita McKimens
11780 SW Queen Elizabeth
King City, OR 97224

*Quantity Discounts are Available